Berlitz®
Kerala

Text by Maria Lord
Photography by: Britta Jaschinski
Series Editor: Tony Hallida~~

D1374458

Berlitz POCKET GUIDE

Kerala

First Edition 2006

PHOTOGRAPHY CREDITS
All pictures Britta Jaschinski/Apa except pages: 19, 20 Private Collection/The Bridgeman Art Library; 48 Walter Imber/Apa; 81 Fayaz A. Mir. Cover picture: Richard Lewisohn/Alamy.

CONTACTING THE EDITORS
Every effort has been made to provide accurate information in this publication, but changes are inevitable. The publisher cannot be responsible for any resulting loss, inconvenience or injury. We would appreciate it if readers would call our attention to any errors or outdated information by contacting Berlitz Publishing, PO Box 7910, London SE1 1WE, England. Fax: (44) 20 7403 0290; e-mail: berlitz@apaguide.co.uk www.berlitzpublishing.com

All Rights Reserved

© 2006 Apa Publications GmbH & Co. *Verlag KG, Singapore Branch, Singapore*

Printed in Singapore by Insight Print Services (Pte) Ltd, 38 Joo Koon Road, Singapore 628990.
Tel: (65) 6865-1600. Fax: (65) 6861-6438

Berlitz Trademark Reg. U.S. Patent Office and other countries. Marca Registrada

The Backwaters (page 36). Perhaps the most beautiful region of Kerala, with limpid waters and palm trees

Kovalam (page 32) i a splendid series of beaches with swimmable water, loved by both locals and visitors

Padmanabhapuram (page 35) is a fine royal palace

TOP TEN ATTRACTIONS

Varkala (page 33) is not as crowded as Kovalam and has wonderful cliff-top views ▼

Kochi (page 44) is a historic city with spices, palaces and a lovely synagogue ◀

Munnar (page 59), with the fabulous landscapes of the Western Ghats, from mountains to tea fields ▶

Bekal (page 79), where a rugged fort juts out into the Indian Ocean ◀

Thrissur and Guruvayur (page 63), the location of Kerala's most important Hindu shrines ▶

Thiruvananthapuram, the state capital, is home to the extraordinary Sri Padmanabhasvami Temple (page 26) ▼

Periyar (page 57), Kerala's most successful national park ▶

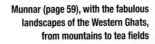

CONTENTS

A ➤ in the text denotes a highly recommended sight

Fact Sheets

INTRODUCTION

Kerala has attracted the attention of traders and travellers for centuries, and indeed many of its religions and much of its money have come from overseas. It was in Kerala that Judaism, Christianity and Islam all first reached India and the region has long been known as a source of spices and wealth. It is thought that one of the reasons for the decline of the Roman Empire was excessive trade with southern India, in which huge amounts of gold were traded for spices (some of the gold still worn by Indian women is thought to have originated in Rome).

Today Kerala still looks abroad to ensure that wealth feeds back into the state, though nowadays this means migrant workers in the Gulf rather than the arrival of Roman galleys or Arab dhows. Keralans also maintain an admirable degree of tolerance towards each other's beliefs.

Kerala's rather conservative outlook extends to its film industry (which elsewhere in India has tended to push social and sexual boundaries). Characters tend to dress in modest and local fashions and the outcome demanded by audiences favours the happy ending of a traditional wedding.

However, for all that Kerala has traditionally welcomed visitors and maintained extensive links with the outside world, it has also been fiercely protective of its own traditions. Compared to some other regions of India, and particularly the large urban areas, it has retained a much more traditional outlook, in terms of dress, religious values and cultural activity.

Paddling through the Backwaters

Even though with 31.8 million people Kerala is one of the most densely populated of all Indian states, and one with the fewest natural resources, it is the most successful in terms of gender equality, family planning and literacy. This is partly due to the resourcefulness of the Malayalis (named after the state language of Malayalam) but also to long-standing and proud traditions of universal education.

Joys and Frustrations

Kerala's traditional outlook is both one of the delights and, perhaps, frustrations of visiting the state. There is still a decorous courtesy towards visitors and the chances of encountering traditional forms of festivity and entertainment are high. Indeed, Kerala's cultural identity has been pushed hard by the state tourism authority as one of its selling points. At the same time, there is, paradoxically given its history, a certain insularity to Keralan society, and it can sometimes be hard for visitors to get beyond the surface of palm trees, backwaters and mediated dance-dramas.

> **Kerala's literacy rate is the highest in India at 90.9 percent (the national average is 64.8). There is also, unlike elsewhere in India, little difference between the rates of male and female literacy.**

Nowhere can this sense of distance be felt more than at the state's many Hindu temples. Access to these large and fascinating buildings is strictly forbidden to non-Hindus, and notices and temple guards are often posted at the entrance to make sure that no-one who should not be there gets beyond the gate. In some particularly sacred temple towns, such as Guruvayur or Thrissur, you may not feel particularly welcome and visitors should try and maintain a respectful distance from both the temples and devotees.

The Western Ghats seen from Eravikulam National Park

Geography

The smallest of the four South Indian states, Kerala is just over 39,000 sq km (15,000 sq miles) in area. The state stretches along the Malabar coast of southwestern India, and nowhere is more than 120km (75 miles) from the shoreline. All along the coast are a series of palm-fringed beaches, behind which in the southern part of the state are the famed Backwaters. These are a huge complex of brackish lagoons and canals, fed by waters running from the mountains. The dappled green waters overhung by coconuts palms are justly one of the great attractions of Kerala. There is a lesser-known series of backwaters in the north of the state.

Another, literal, high point is the Western Ghats. This forest-clad spine of mountains runs the whole length of Kerala, broken only by the Palakkad Gap roughly midway through the state. They rise to a height of 2,694m (8,842ft) at the peak of Anaimudi, South India's highest mountain.

**Radha and Krishna from a mural
on a traditional Nair house**

Home to a number of national parks and sanctuaries, including one of the last pockets of primary rainforest in India, they are also economically important as their height is perfect for growing tea, fields of which clad many of the slopes.

Lying some 200–300km (120–190 miles) off the Keralan coast are the Lakshadweep islands, a low-lying archipelago, the only true coral islands owned by India. Surrounded by reefs, which enclose shallow lagoons, and set in glitteringly clear seas, the islands are part of the same chain as the Maldives which lie further to the south. Although the Lakshadweep islands are not part of the state, the predominately Muslim population are Malayalam speakers and have strong links with the Keralan mainland.

Climate

Lying well within the tropics, Kerala is hot all year round. Average winter temperatures are around 25°C (77°F), rising to a maximum of 33°C (91°F) during the summer months (April–May). Subject to the monsoon and with an annual rainfall exceeding 2.54m (100 in) in several districts, Kerala is green and lush throughout the year. The southwestern monsoon arrives in late May with the wet period continuing up to September, while there is a later period of lighter rains (the northeastern monsoon) during October to December.

Migrant Workers and Gulf Houses

The high level of literacy (which was due in great part to the enlightened educational policies of the hereditary rulers of Travancore), coupled with few employment opportunities in Kerala itself, has led to Keralans finding work all over India and in the Gulf states. Gulf workers in particular have proved an important source of income for the state, sending much of their money home to their families. Evidence for this can be seen in the proliferation of 'Gulf

The Religious Complex

In terms of religion, Kerala might well be the most heterogenous Indian state. It has, over the past 2,000 years, been home to Hindus, Jews, Christians, Muslims and worshippers of Adivasi (literally 'indigenous') deities. In contrast to some other regions of India, relations between the different communities have been, and continue to be, largely peaceful. Perhaps this is because the arrival of the different beliefs was gradual and came through trade and refugees fleeing persecution rather than invasion.

Kerala is a Hindu majority state (around 52 percent of the population), yet its two large minority communities, the Muslims (26 percent), and Christians (19 percent), have made a huge impact on its history, and its cultural and physical geography. It is claimed that Chrsitianity arrived in Kerala in around AD60 with the apostle Thomas. However, it has certainly been present since the 6th century when Orthodox Syrian missionaries arrived. There have been many splits and schisms since then and numerous different churches exist under the broad heading of 'Syrian Christian'. Islam arrived in Kerala with Arab traders in the late-7th century. They subsequently settled along the coast. Known locally as the Mapillas, they are still a significant presence in coastal communities, particularly in the north of the state.

Umbrellas at Kovalam beach

houses', some of them extraordinary fantasies, with Corinthian columns, sweeping staircases and huge satellite dishes, all built of concrete in defiance of the climate and environment. The true heartland of Gulf architecture is in the north of the state, but it can be seen wherever migrant workers have returned.

Women

Women in Kerala have traditionally had a higher profile than elsewhere in India. Some communities, predominantly the Nairs, practised matrilineal inheritance and women were in charge of family property. Although this has now largely ended, its legacy and high literacy rates have empowered Keralan women and they tend to have more freedom than their counterparts in other states. This is also one of the very few Indian states where women outnumber men as, unlike elsewhere in India, female foeticide is practically unknown.

Dance-Dramas

Kerala is home to a myriad of local art forms, of which some of the most spectacular are its dance-dramas. The most famous of these, and one which has now almost become synonymous with the state, is *Kathakali*. Immediately noticeable from its lavish make-up and costumes, it is a highly complex genre that presents stories from the Ramayana, the Mahabarata and other Hindu epics. The characters fall into five main types, and the make-up distinguishes these types (green stands for good, red for evil and white for a deity). While owing much to ancient Sanskrit drama, it has during its history absorbed many other elements of ritual, some local, such as *Teyyam (see page 78)*, and of Keralan martial arts (specifically *Kalaripayattu*).

Allied to *Kathakali* is the Sanskrit drama *Kutiyattam*. This is the only continuing South Asian performance art that adheres closely to the precepts laid down in Bharata's *Natyasastra* (circa 4th century AD), the earliest extant treatise on music and drama. A temple art performed traditionally by a specific community, *Kutiyattam* embraces elements of music and dance as well as pure spoken drama.

A *Teyyam* dancer

The performers use make-up similar to *Kathakali* but are permitted speech, albeit in a stylised manner. A very complex form, it can be several days or even weeks before a *Kutiyattam* drama cycle is completed.

Mohini Attam, a solo dance form, was established by Svati Tirunal in the early 19th century and revived again in the 1930s. Not widely performed outside of Kerala, unlike the other classical dances of the state which are traditionally restricted to men, it is a female dance form in which the striking feature is the rhythmic swaying of the dancer from side to side.

A BRIEF HISTORY

Although surrounded neatly by its geography from neighbouring areas, the history of Kerala is complex. Indeed geography has aided this complexity as the region has both tended to look outwards and receive visitors from the sea as well as take its part in historical currents elsewhere in South India. The land that became Kerala was visited by Phonecians, Greeks and Romans, then the Arabs, the Jews and the Chinese, and then – following Vasco da Gama's route – the Portuguese, the Danes, the Dutch, the French and the English.

Early History

The early history of Kerala has a number of different streams, from the archaeological to the mythological, in particular the creation myth of Parasurama *(see panel)*. Archaeological and architectural evidence of earlier settlements is lacking in Kerala. Most structures have traditionally been made of wood and so have been lost to rot and termite damage.

The roots of Kerala's creation lie in myth. After doing penance Parasurama (an incarnation of Vishnu) was given leave to find somewhere to live by seeing how far he could throw his mace. He threw it from Kanniyakumari to Gokarna, and thus established the land of Kerala.

The first settlements in Kerala were possibly established during the Neolithic, evidenced by the discovery of megaliths and urn burials. The construction of megalithic monuments seems to have continued during the copper and bronze ages.

Numismatics tell us little about the early history of Kerala. Inscriptions of the 9th–13th centuries refer to coinage, but there is little

Traditional woodcarving at Padmanabhapuram Palace

precise way of dating the coins discovered. Roman coins (dating between 30BC and AD547) have also been discovered, suggesting that trade with Rome continued for almost 600 years. The Phoenicians are thought to have visited the southern Keralan coast in around 1000BC, though no record remains of what they found there.

The first Jews arrived on the Keralan coast after the Romans sacked the temple in Jerusalem in AD70, thus beginning a long tradition of persecuted peoples finding sanctuary in Kerala. Christians date the advent of their religion in South Asia to the supposed arrival of St Thomas the Apostle near Kodungallur in AD52, though it is known for certain that orthodox Syrian Christian missionaries arrived in Kerala during the 6th century.

The Cheras
The principal evidence for reconstructing the early history of Kerala comes from the Tamil Sangam literature and copper-

plate inscriptions. The language used on these inscriptions is almost always an early form of Malayalam but written in Vatteluttu (an early Tamil script). From these sources it appears that the northern part of the state, after some early contact with the Mauryan Empire of Asoka during which it is thought that the first wider organisation of society took place, fell under the influence of the Tamil Cheras, and it is likely that it is they who traded with Romans. The Greek geographer Ptolemy (1st century AD) described the region of Aioi, which stretched from the River Pampa to Kanniyakumari. This has been equated with the area ruled by the Ay dynasty, who controlled the region around Thiruvananthapuram up until the 10th century.

The year 925 seems to have been the end of the Ay kingdom and it is likely that it had been taken over by the Chera Empire to the north. Around this time Brahmans, moving in

India's oldest mosque, Kodungallur

from Tamil country, started to found settlements in Kerala. This not only established a much more structured caste system in the region, but also, as this system of social organisation adapted itself to local conditions, marked the move away from the influence of the Tamils and the emergence of Malayali culture and Malayalam as a language.

The rulers of the kingdom of Venad (based in Kollam) were under the control of the Chera Empire, whose capital was in Mahodayapuram (present-day Kodungallur). Venad was the southernmost reach of Chera influence. There is evidence to suggest that up until the 12th century the rule of Venad was not hereditary, but in the hands of the Chera ruler of the time.

The Arrival of Islam

It is thought that Islam came to Kerala in the 7th century AD through interaction with Arabs who had been trading for centuries with what they called Malabar. Malik ibn Dinar, one of the companions of the Prophet, visited Kerala during the 7th century. As well as the mosque at Kodungallur, he is said to have established nine other mosques which are still extant, including those at Chaliyam near Beypore, Kollam, Madayi near Kannur and Ezhimalai near Kasaragode. These are all coastal towns, pointing to the close connection between maritime trade and the arrival of Islam. The Kerala Muslims, called Mapillas, grew as a community by inter-marriage with Arab traders and the religion gradually spread by precept and practice, not compulsion.

Things Fall Apart

The 12th century marks a crucial point in the history of Kerala. Attacks on the Cheras from the Cholas and Pandyas from present-day Tamil Nadu led to the Chera *Perumal* (king) Rama Kulasekhara fleeing to the Arabian Gulf. This left a power vacuum in which the divisions of the Chera Empire (roughly northern, central and southern Kerala) began to establish their own borders and ruling families. Each of these soon-to-be-established dynasties would claim descent from the Chera *perumals*.

In the north of the state the *Eradis* (or governors) moved their capital down onto the coast and in time they became known as the Zamorins of Kozhikode. This was to become the most powerful of the Keralan kingdoms and it sought to take over the lands of the Raja of Kochi, the smallest of the three states, during the 13th–15th century. In the south it was the Kingdom of Venad that established itself as the ruling house, though the fledgling state was overrun several times by competing powers until its borders were consolidated by Ravi Varma Kulasekhara in the early 14th century. Ravi Varma was credited with being a great scholar and musician, like his descendent Svati Tirunal *(see page 21)*.

The Portuguese

In 1498, a complicating factor in the relations between the three states emerged when the Portuguese navigator Vasco da Gama landed near Kozhikode. At first the Zamorin greeted him warmly and granted the Portuguese the same trading rights accorded to other peoples along the coast.

This, it turned out, was not enough for the Portuguese, and too much for the Arab traders who had traditionally supported the Zamorin in his battles with the neighbouring state of Kochi. Before long war had broken out between the Zamorin and Arabs on one side and the Portuguese and the Raja of Kochi on the other. The ensuing battles were fierce and shifting loyalties meant that the Portuguese were ensured a substantial presence in Kerala until the early 17th century.

Although they only had a hold over the central part of the state for around 100 years, their influence was considerable, not least on the indigenous Syrian Christians. The Portuguese tried to 'Latinise' local practices, a process that caused a great deal of heated argument. This was eventually partially resolved in the rebellion of the Coonan Cross (still to be found in Kochi, not far from the Mattancherri Palace). At this place in 1653 local Syrian Christians tied themselves to the cross and vowed to resist all attempts to make them worship Rome, and to remain true to the Patriarch of Antioch and the Syriac rites which missionaries had brought over in the 6th century; the dispute still rumbles on today.

Vasco da Gama

The Dutch and British

The Portuguese met their downfall with the arrival of the Dutch. In 1603 the Dutch East India Company signed a treaty with the Zamorin of Kozhikode to help him get rid of the Portuguese. By 1662 they had captured Kodungallur, and the following year they entered Fort Kochi. Here they set up a puppet king and by the beginning of the 18th century they had control over the entire state of Kochi.

However, the Dutch met their nemeses in the shapes of Haider Ali and the British. While the British had had a trade agreement with the Zamorin since 1615, and had built a factory (warehouse) near Vizinjam to the south of Thiruvananthapuram in 1644, they had not advanced much further. It was the invasions by Haider Ali, ruler of the Mysore state who was

Pagodas at Calicut, early 19th-century British engraving

conducting a campaign against the British in the Madras Presidency, that gave the British their chance.

In 1776 the British helped the Zamorin beat back Haider Ali, and with this foothold proceeded to take over the entire region. By 1791 Kochi was paying tribute to the British, and in 1795 the British invaded the state, driving the Dutch out of South Asia. Malabar, nominally under the control of the Zamorin, became part of the Madras Presidency in 1801, and through treaties in 1795 and 1805 the state of Travancore (as Venad had become) came under the purview of British rule.

Independence

At first there were rebellions against this imposition of colonial power. Pazhassi Raja led a powerful revolt against the British in northern Kerala between 1793 and 1805, and in Travancore the British were forced to invade in 1809 against a declaration of independence (the ruler soon backed down). Thereafter things quietened down and for the most part the two states of Travancore and Kochi were left to their own devices.

Local meetings of the Indian National Congress began in 1904, and a later meeting of representatives from across the region in 1921. This year also saw the Mapilla Uprising, when Muslims in northern Kerala rioted after police opened fire on a demonstration in support of the Gandhi-inspired Non-Cooperation Movement.

One movement that was to have a lasting effect was Aikya Kerala, which formed in 1928 and demanded the creation of a united Malayalam region. In another development that was to bear fruit later, left-wing activists began to group together within the Congress Party, recieving a great deal of support from workers and peasant farmers. In 1939 they broke away and joined the Communist Party. Meanwhile, the enlightened rajas of Travancore instigated universal education and, in 1938, issued the Temple Entry Proclamation, which ensured freedom of entry to all Hindus regardless of caste.

A Musical Dynasty

The Travancore royal family is a bit of an exception among the world's ruling dynasties in having a keen interest in culture. Much of their interest in patronage of the arts stems from the early-19th century ruler, Svati Tirunal (1813–47). During his short life he became one of the most respected of South Indian performers and composers, and he turned Travancore into a musical centre to rival that of Thanjavur in Tamil Nadu (the other great centre of *Karnatak* music of the time). Svati Tirunals compositions are a mainstay of the *Karnatak* repertory and are still often heard in concerts. The royal family still maintains its musicial traditions, sponsoring two annual music festivals in Thiruvananthapuram (one in early January and the other at Navaratri), and Prince Rama Varma, nephew of the current *Maharaja*, is a respected *vina* player.

Modern Kerala

The contemporary face of Kerala: M.G. Road, Ernakulam

After the British left India in 1947, Kerala was still divided between the two princely states of Travancore, Cochin and the Malabar regions of the Madras Presidency. With the reorganisation of states along linguistic lines, these were combined, and in 1956 the modern state of Kerala came into being.

During the state's first elections in 1957, Keralans voted for the world's first democratically elected Communist government. This was controversially dismissed by the Congress government in Delhi after intense lobbying by Indira Gandhi. The CPI(M) (Communist Party of India, Marxist), which soon regained power with a huge popular mandate, was led by the great E.M.S. Namboodiripad (known simply as 'EMS'), who pushed through sweeping land reform, educational and health care programmes.

Contemporary Keralan politics is a complex business, with around 32 political parties, and the state has been alternately ruled by the faction-ridden Congress or the Marxists. The Left Democratic Front, led by the CPI(M), won the 2006 state assembly elections with a large majority.

Contemporary Keralan society is as complex as it politics, with growing modern cities and increasing problems in rural areas. It has not been immune from the forces of nature either: in 2004 the Asian tsunami hit the Keralan coast, killing hundreds of people.

Historical Landmarks

1000BC The Phoenicians trade with peoples of the Keralan coast.

1st–12th century AD The Ay Kingdom rules southern Kerala and the Chera Empire controls the north, taking over from the Ays in the south from the 10th century.

AD52 St Thomas the Apostle arrives in Kodungallur.

AD70 Jews fleeing persecution arrive in Kerala.

7th century Malik ibn Dinar founds the first mosque in India.

12th century Attacks from the Cholas and Pandyas destroy the Chera Empire, the three kingdoms of Travancore (southern Kerala), Kochi (central Kerala) and Malabar (northern Kerala) begin to emerge.

1498 Vasco da Gama lands near Kozhikode.

1603 The Dutch make a treatise with the Zamorin of Kozhikode.

1653 The rebellion of the Coonan Cross.

1663 The Dutch capture Kochi.

1776 The British help the Zamorin fight Haider Ali.

1793–1805 Pazhassi Raja leads a freedom struggle against the Britsh in northern Malabar.

1795 The British invade Kochi.

1795–1805 Travancore pledges allegiance to the British.

1801 The British incorporate Malabar into the Madras Presidency.

1809 Travancore is invaded after they declare independence.

1904 The first meeting of the Indian National Congress in Kerala.

1921 The Mapilla Uprising in northern Malabar.

1928 Calls for a united Malayalam-speaking region.

1938 The Maharaja of Travancore's Temple Entry Proclamation opens the doors of temples to all Hindus, regardless of caste.

1939 Left-wing activists leave Congress and join the Communists.

1947 India becomes Independent.

1956 The modern state of Kerala comes into being.

1957 Kerala votes for the world's first democratically elected communist government.

2004 The Asian tsunami hits the Keralan coast.

WHERE TO GO

Kerala packs a lot into a relatively little space, from beaches and palm-fringed backwaters to historic city and temple sites to rainforest sanctuaries and high mountains. Everywhere you will be overwhelmed by just how green the state is, be it the palm trees that line the coast, the waters of the inland lagoons and canals or the bright leaves of the tea plantations of the Western Ghats.

Most visitors arrive in the far south of the state, near to the beaches of Kovalam and Varkala, and then travel north through the Backwaters to the historic city of Kochi. Beyond lies the sacred heartland of Hindu Kerala and the little-explored far north. Running the whole length of the state are the mountains, covered in tea plantations and thick forest.

> **The name Thiruvananthapuram means 'holy city of Ananda'. Ananda is the many-headed snake that the god Vishnu reclines on in the main temple of the city.**

THIRUVANANTHAPURAM

The main entry point into Kerala is Thiruvananthapuram (previously Trivandrum). It is also one of the loveliest capital cities in the country – small, green and clean. Many visitors will head straight to Kovalam *(see page 32)* but it would be a shame to miss the city's temple, palace and museums. The city is easily reached from Kovalam (either by bus or auto-rickshaw) and for those who don't like the busy nightlife of Kovalam it can make a pleasant alternative base from which to visit the beach.

The Sri Padmanabhasvami Temple

Fort

The oldest part of the city is delineated by the old laterite wall of the Fort (only parts of the walls now remain) to the southwest of the railway station. This was the core of royal Thiruvananthapuram, containing the city's main temple and the royal palace. At the centre of the fort is a large tank, leading away from which there are roads lined with traditional shops and small houses.

Sri Padmanabhasvami Temple

The **Sri Padmanabhasvami Temple** dominates the Fort district. This Vishnu temple with a seven-storey *gopuram* (the impressively decorated entrance tower) is not representative of Keralan architecture, but is built in the Dravidian style of neighbouring Tamil Nadu. As such it is unique in the state, both in its scale and the degree of its embellishments. The

The decorative gable over the temple entrance

temple overlooks the large temple tank (lake or pool used by the devotees for washing) known as the Padma Tirtham.

Young pilgrims peer from a bus window

It is said that the image housed inside the inner sanctum was found in a nearby forest. Over the years the temple grew, till in the 18th century the princely state of Travancore, the southernmost part of Kerala, was dedicated to its deity. Since then, the rights and the possessions of its rulers have belonged to the deity, and the maharajas of Travancore are considered only the regents of the deity. The hereditary rulers of Travancore, while they have no temporal power, do still run the affairs of the temple and take part in important rituals.

The temple is only open to Hindus (and then only those who adhere to its dress code of a sari for women and a *dhoti* for men) and admission is strictly forbidden to anyone else. However, the temple attendants are generally friendly and will allow you to look through the gates for a glimpse of the inside. The entrance corridor (known as the *Sivalimanlapam*, 'the walk of the god's procession') is beautiful, lined with statues of Nair women holding lamps. The central shrine is surrounded by a walkway, and in front is a large gold-covered pole which can be glimpsed from the outside. Inside the main shrine is an image of Vishnu (here known as Sri Padmanabha) reclining on the snake Ananda. Those Hindu visitors who enter the temple to do *puja* (worship the god) should not miss the exceptionally fine granite carving in the adjacent Kulasekhara Mandapam.

Puttan Malika Palace

The Government Ayurvedic College just off M.G. Road was established over 100 years ago. It was the first in India and still trains many of the Ayurvedic doctors and nurses working in the state today.

The maharajas of Travancore moved their capital to Thiruvananthapuram from Padmanabhapuram in 1790 and took up residence alongside the temple on the southern side of its tank. The **Puttan Malika Palace** (open Tues–Sun 8.30am–1pm, 3–5.30pm) was their city residence. You must take off your shoes and go around with a guide (a small tip is appreciated). The attractive wooden-built structure – very cool in the summer heat – is set in quiet gardens and contains a number of royal possessions, including an ivory cradle, Svati Tirunal's ivory throne and a large collection of weapons.

However, it is the building itself that is most impressive, with beautifully carved ceilings and the two delightful end rooms on the upper storey. The one nearest the temple was Svati Tirunal's composing room *(see panel on page 21)* whilst at the other end is the 'Dancing Hall', linked by a corridor decorated on the outside by 122 horses carved in teak.

Leaving the Fort, head east to the large gateway opposite the temple. This contains a helpful office of the Archaeological Survey of India who can give you information on the sights of the city. Crossing the busy road brings you to East Fort. Here is the stand from where you catch the bus to Kovalam. Beyond is the traditional shopping district of **Chala Bazaar**, and this is where the city's main fruit and vegetable market can be found, along with small shops huddled together down narrow roads selling just about anything. Temporary fairs and exhibitions are often held on the piece of open ground beside the bus stand.

M.G. Road

The modern city lies to the north of the railway. Opposite the railway station, by the main bus stand, is Laurie Baker's intriguing spiral building for the Indian Coffee House, a good place to stop for a snack or light meal. Laurie Baker is a British architect who made Kerala his home and propagated a low-cost style of architecture that blended the traditional with the modern.

M.G. Road, which runs north from the railway, is the city's main street. Always full of traffic and so rather polluted, it is lined with banks, shops and official buildings (including the central post office). About halfway along is the impressive State Secretariat, built in the mid-19th century in a classical style, at Statue Junction. This is usually surrounded by groups demanding action on a whole series of causes, while opposite are a couple of good places in which to eat.

Busy city streets seen from an auto-rickshaw

Between M.G. Road and Aristo Road, to the east, is a series of narrow streets which, while not containing anything of specific interest, are delightful and fun to explore. Carrying on north on M.G. Road leads to Spencer Junction where there is the Orthodox cathedral and, opposite, a useful supermarket. Just beyond, at Palayam Junction, surrounded by rambling 19th-centruy buildings set in large grounds, are the impressive **Victoria Jubilee Town Hall** and the neo-Gothic Catholic **St Joseph's Cathedral**, and the Anglican Christ Church built in 1859. Beyond these are many of the Indo-Saracenic buildings of the university.

Public Park

M.G. Road ends at Museum Road, lining which is Thiruvananthapuram's beautifully laid-out Botanical Gardens. Here is the city's museum, consisting of: the **Art Museum**

The extraordinary Indo-Saracenic Art Museum

(previously the Napier Museum), the **Sri Chitra Art Gallery**, the **Paniker Gallery** and the **Museum of Natural History** (all are open Tues, Thur–Sun 10am–4.30pm, Wed 1–4.30pm). A combined ticket for the museums is available from the booth near the entrance for the city zoo.

Side saddle on a bike

The sprawling gardens with their wealth of plant life are far more attractive than the depressing zoo with its poorly caged animals. A better view of local natural history can be found in the Museum of Natural History which, as well as various pickled snakes, marine specimens washed up on the city's beaches and unfortunate stuffed birds and animals which fell foul of colonial hunters, has informative displays of local costume and an excellent model of a *tharavad*, the traditional home of a Nair community joint family.

Art Galleries

The highlight of the museum complex is the Art Museum (Napier Museum), housed in an extraordinary Indo-Saracenic building designed by Robert Fellowes Chisolm for Lord Napier in 1880; its many gables and sloped roofs fuse the traditional architecture of Kerala with a British Colonial style. It has a superb collection which includes jewellery, ivorywork, Chola bronzes and Keralan woodcarvings.

The Sri Chitra Art Gallery has several good Chinese and Japanese paintings, a series of Tibetan *thankas* (religious paintings), and a surprising number of works by Nicholas and Svetoslav Roerich who painted mystical scenes of the

Lighthouse Beach, Kovalam

Himalayas. The bulk of the collection, however, is the work of Raja Ravi Varma (1848–1906), a member of the Travancore royal family and considered one of India's finest painters. His rather academic paintings are based for the most part on Hindu themes and they can still be seen in reproduction all over India; they are a little syrupy for modern tastes.

Also in the grounds is a gallery given over to a collection of works by the 20th-century South Indian artist K.C.S. Paniker (1911–77), some of whose early paintings are quite charming.

Sanmukam and Veli

Thiruvananthapuram does have its own beach, out near the airport. **Sanmukam Beach** is not a place for swimming or sunbathing (the sea is rough and the sand rather dirty), but it is a good place for a stroll and very popular with local families and couples. North along the coast road is **Veli Tourist Village**, a park with a playground for children and a lake on which you can go boating.

Kovalam

Many visitors to Thiruvananthapuram, however, come in quest of Kerala's beaches, and **Kovalam**, 15km (9 miles) to the south, is one of the best. Be warned, however, that it is no longer idyllic and quiet. During the high season it has the appearance of a Spanish resort and the beach is lined with concrete hotels, eating places and shops selling overpriced souvenirs. However, the better, and quieter, beaches to the north are still well worth a visit.

The southernmost beach, known as Lighthouse Beach, is the busiest, if perhaps the one with the best stretch of sand. Well-policed by lifeguards the swimming here is generally safe, at least outside of the monsoon. Here you will find all the tourist facilities you might want, and even if it has been taken over by tourists, fishermen still pull their catch in onto the sands. Hawa Beach is the next stretch to the north. Separated by a small promontory from Lighthouse Beach it is still very busy. For a better experience head for Ashok Beach, over the hill at the north end of Hawa Beach. This is the quietest of the three and much more laid-back.

Just to the south of Kovalam, beyond the lighthouse, is the fishing port of Vizhinjam. Now very much a working port, with all the resultant sleaze and dirt, it was once the capital of the Ay dynasty, though there are no visible remains of their city. The beach beyond the port is much more pleasant, backed by palm trees and with rows of brightly painted fishing boats.

Watching the sunset at Varkala

Beaches and Temples

➤ **Varkala** (46km/28 miles north of Thiruvananthapuram), known to travellers for its beautiful beach, is one of Kerala's major Hindu pilgrim centres. The Janardana temple here is believed to be over 2,000 years old. Its bell is said to be from a 17th-century Dutch sailing ship whose captain gave it to the temple when his prayers were answered. The mineral springs here are much sought-after for their curative properties.

Also in Varkala is Sivagiri Hill, where Narayana, the Keralan philosopher-saint, established an *ashram*. The *ashram* and the social reformer's *samadhi* (sanctified tomb) attract many pilgrims.

The beach of Varkala has become popular, not only with locals, but also with those backpackers who dislike the commercialism and crowds of Kovalam. The red cliffs are a superb place from which to watch the sunset (cafés and restaurants line the cliff top from where you get a good vantage point). However, like at Kovalam, the sea can be dangerous here. Lifeguards are posted on the beach but you should be careful not to swim outside of the flags and not to go out too far.

The Pumukham at Padmanabhapuram

Padmanabhapuram

Until Independence and the reorganisation of the princely states, much of this coastal strip was part of the erstwhile kingdom of Travancore, now southern Kerala. From the mid-16th to the late-18th century the

> **The palace has its own air-cooling system. The arrangement of wooden louvres in the palace keeps out direct sunlight and their curved shape encourages the flow of air around the rooms.**

capital of Travancore was not Thiruvananthapuram but the palace of **Padmanabhapuram**, 55km (34 miles) to the south, and now in the neighbouring state of Tamil Nadu.

The **palace** (open Tues–Sun 9am–1pm, 2–4.30pm) can easily be reached by bus, train (to Eraniel) or taxi from Thiruvananthapuram, and the state tourist authority runs tours here which also take in Kanyakumari, at the very southernmost tip of India (Tues–Sun). It sits at the centre of a small village, which now thrives on selling food and drinks to visitors, and the main entrance leads into a large courtyard where there is the ticket office and a small Museum of Antiquities (open 9am–5pm).

The palace is spread out over a large rectangular plan and it forms a warren of halls, passageways and small courtyards. The first building entered is the Pumukham (literally 'flower's face', *see left*), a wonderfully decorated pagoda-type building that held the kings' council chamber. Here you can see small panes of mica set into the windows which cast a coloured light into the cool rooms.

Although the whole palace is beautifully finished and with many fine examples of woodcarving, particular sights to look out for include the Thaikkottaram (the oldest building in the complex) and the Uppirikka Malika (literally 'multi-storeyed building') which has a superb series of murals based on the Hindu stories of the Puranas.

THE BACKWATERS

The region north of Thiruvananthapuram is known as Kuttanad, home to the famous **Backwaters**. A special delight is the trip on a slow boat through the palm-shaded lagoons and canals, enjoying magnificent scenery along the waterways and stopping to admire what history and religion have left in many towns and villages on the way. Motor-powered launches provide regular passenger services for locals and tourists alike, but the same experience in a covered country boat, known as a *kettuvallam (see panel on page 84)* is also a lovely experience. The boat design is due to the Chinese influence on this coast.

**Quiet settlements like this
line the Backwaters**

In theory it is possible to make a journey by boat from Thiruvananthapuram to either Kodungallur (some 250km/155 miles), or to Kottayam (175km/110 miles), but the classic journey is between the towns of Kollam (previously Quilon, 70km/44 miles north of Thiruvananthapuram) and Alappuzha (formerly Alleppey). From Alappuzha it is easy to continue your journey up the coast to Kochi by either train or bus.

Two companies run cruises for tourists between the two towns: the state Water Transport Department boats are usually slower than those of Alleppey Tourism. The trip lasts up to eight hours, depending on the route taken and the number of stops (there are usually at least a couple for you to eat and stretch your legs). However, it can be a long day for some travellers who might want to settle for one of the shorter cruises offered by many of the resorts in the area, or for a much more comfortable night or two on board a *kettuvallam*.

Kollam

This now somewhat dreamy little town has long been known as a trading centre. It is thought to have been visited by the Phoenicians, Romans, Arabs and Chinese (who left the design for the distinctive fishing nets that still line the banks of

The ecology of the Backwaters is under threat, not only from land reclamation, but also from the water hyacinth. This aggressive plant, which originates in the Amazon, forms thick blankets of vegetation through which light cannot penetrate. The absence of light kills off the underlying vegetation and the plant's decomposition removes oxygen from the water.

the Backwaters), and it is said that Marco Polo also passed though. It is still one of the major centres of the cashew-nut trade but that has declined, and so has the commercial life of the town.

Even though it has an illustrious history (at one time being the capital of this part of Kerala) there is little to see in Kollam itself, though its location on the banks of the huge Astamudi Lake (the 'lake with eight corners') is lovely. At the centre of the town is Chinakkada Bazaar, still bustling and interesting to look around, while the Roman Catholic cathedral, though the building only dates from 1830, is on the site of the first seat of a Roman Catholic bishop in India. Friar Jordanus was consecrated bishop of Kollam in 1328.

The main boat jetty is conveniently placed near the centre of town, a short auto-rickshaw ride from the railway station.

Thangasseri

About 3km (2 miles) north of Kollam is the small town of **Thangasseri**, which has a number of remains of the colonial era. On the way, in Ashramam, you pass the old British Residency (1810) which is now a delightfully unspoilt government guesthouse on the shores of Ashtamudi Lake. The chief sight in Thangasseri is the lighthouse, one of the first the British built in India (in 1902) and still working. The old Portuguese, Dutch and English cemeteries are quite interesting, as are the scanty remains of the Portuguese fort.

Boat Races

To the north of Kollam the Backwaters stretch all the way to Kochi, in a seemingly unending series of canals and lakes. While for most of the year they are dreamy and quiet during August and September, the banks come to life with cheering spectators for the ***vallam kallis***, or boat races.

The most famous of these is the Nehru Trophy Boat Race, held at Alappuzha on the second Saturday of August every year. There are races for a variety of boats, but the most impressive is for the *chundan vallams*, the giant snake boats. Each boat is over 30-m (100-ft) long, with raised snake-like prows, and is highly decorated; crews number more than 100 men rowing in perfect rhythm to traditional boat songs. Another important snake-boat race takes place at Aranmula on the River Pamba during the festival of Onam (a week-long harvest celebration which falls during August–September).

A local ferry on the Backwaters

The Champakulam snake boat

Alappuzha

North of Kollam, 85km (53 miles) away, is **Alappuzha** (formerly Alleppey), known somewhat optimistically as the 'Venice of the East'. Although in the past it may have been a pleasant coir-trading settlement (coir is the fibre of the coconut husk) spread out between a maze of canals and bridges, it is now a busy and rather polluted commercial port servicing a huge number of *kettuvallams* and ferries. It is, however, situated on Vembanad Lake, the longest lake in India, and close by are some of the most attractive places to stay in the Backwaters region *(see pages 127–8)* making it a good place to stop over after taking the ferry up from Kollam. It is also a convenient place to start your *kettuvallam* cruise, and there are good connections by rail and road on to Kochi.

Champakulam

The Backwaters that stretch south and north from Alappuzha are just as attractive as those around Kollam, and cruises on the *kettuvallam* are a very popular way to see them. Aside from the landscape, there are a number of interesting sights to the south of Alappuzha that many of the boats pass by.

One of these is the small village of **Champakulam**, famous for both its snake boat, the most successful in Kerala, having won the Nehru Trophy three times in a row, and also the wonderful **St Mary's Church**. Built by the Portuguese around 480 years ago, this now Syrian Catholic church has an ornately decorated interior. The vibrant murals, with mixed Hindu and Christian motifs (such as the Apostles surrounded by lotus carvings), are all painted with vegetable dyes, and outside is a gold-covered flagpole, very similar to those found in Hindu temples, a further hint of the mixing of traditions that has taken place in this region.

Ambalapuzha and the Karumadi Kuttan

Also in the region to the south of Alappuzha is the Krishna temple at **Ambalapuzha**. One of the most important Hindu pilgrimage sites in this part of the state, it is said to have been founded when the local king heard the sound of a flute whilst out on the river. Going in search of who was making it, he found a young boy playing the flute in the branches of a pipul tree. This, of course, was the god Krishna, and a temple was founded on the spot where the tree stood. The image inside the shrine, however, is believed to come from elsewhere and the Champakulam boat race (in June–July) celebrates its arrival at the temple.

The half-Buddha Kuttan at Karumadi

Close by, on the riverbank at **Karumadi**, is the rather strange **Kuttan**, an 11th-century black granite statue of the Buddha. One side of the image is missing and it is said that the statue was damaged when it was accidentally knocked into by a passing elephant.

Kottayam

Northeast of Alappuzha, and close to the eastern side of Vembanad Lake, is the prosperous city of **Kottayam**. This is one of the great bastions of Syrian Christianity in Kerala and there are many churches in the city. As well as being an important commercial centre (it derives much of its wealth from trade in rubber, tea, coffee, pepper and cardamom grown in

---

The Sabrimala Pilgrimage

Sabrimala, the temple of Lord Ayappa, is approached from Kottayam along a road that curves up to the Pamba River. A 5-km (3-mile) trek from the river through thick forest brings you to a hill temple. During the main festival season in November–January the path is thronged with pilgrims (overwhelmingly male – women between the ages of 10 and 50 are not allowed to climb the hill). During the days leading up to the Sabrimala festival, a common sight in South Indian cities is the large number of men wearing black *lungis*, a sign of their devotion. Over the past 20 or so years the number of pilgrims has increased dramatically from around 10,000 to between 150–200,000 people, making it one of the busiest sites in India.

Each pilgrim takes the vow of abstinence at a local temple. The period of penance lasts 41 days, during which they dress in black, eat vegetarian food and abstain from sex. The pilgrimage itself takes a week. Each devotee takes a bag with two compartments, which is worn on the head. In one half is a coconut filled with *ghi*, an offering to the god, in the other is rice, a sugar ball and a stick of camphor.

There are two routes up to the shrine. The longest, and most holy because it was the one taken by Aiyappa himself, starts at Erumeli and is about 72km (45 miles). The alternative, and much shorter, route which starts at Chalakayam is the one taken by the majority of pilgrims. As they trek towards the temple they chant the name of the god, *Svamiye Saranam Ayappa*.

the Western Ghats), the city has a long and proud history of education and publishing. It claims the highest literacy rate in Kerala (though the figure given of 100 percent should be taken with a pinch of salt), is the centre of the Keralan publishing industry and was the first city to produce a daily newspaper in Malayalam, the Malayala Manorama founded in 1888 and still the most widely

Both young and old are at home on the water

read paper in the state (the English-language version on their website <www.manoramaonline.com> is a great source of information).

The two most important churches in Kottayam are **St Mary's Valiapalli**, built by local Christians in 1550, and **St Mary's Cheriapalli**, founded by the Portuguese. They are both decorated with colourful frescoes and in St Mary's Valiapalli there are two crosses (from the 4th–7th century) with Pahlavi inscriptions (the language of Sassanid Persia).

Kumarakom

Ten kilometres (6 miles) to the west of Kottayam is **Kumarakom** on the eastern shore of Vembanad Lake. This is a popular holiday destination and the colonial Baker's Bungalow is now an expensive hotel. As well as the beautiful surroundings, the lake shore around Kumarakom has been turned into a bird sanctuary, which can be explored on foot. The lake attracts a large variety of waders – herons and storks – as well as a large number of migratory species during November and February.

KOCHI-ERNAKULAM

The joint city of Kochi-Ernakulam (formerly Cochin) is the commercial capital of Kerala. It is a city of peninsulas and islands with the commercial centre on the mainland. Kochi has a magnificent natural harbour, almost in the middle of the city, which separates it from Ernakulam. It was created by the underwater Malabar mud banks that ensure calm waters for ships loading and offloading their cargoes.

These watery surroundings mean that getting between the different parts of the city almost always involves a ferry ride, and the small boats that criss-cross the harbour are one of the distinctive features of city life. Riding on them you pass huge bulk carriers and tankers, pass long lines of colonial warehouses and get an unparalleled view of the city's skyline. Another distinctive element to Kochi and its history is the spice trade. It has always attracted traders (and so Western colonial adventurers) in search of the 'black gold' of Malabar, as pepper was known, and although the trade is now on the decline you can still find *godowns* (the local word for a warehouse) full of pungent-smelling sacks in the atmospheric backstreets of the old city.

> **Kochi has long been a magnet for traders. As well as drawing on local designs, its architecture shows influences of each successive arrival, from the Portuguese to the Dutch to the British.**

Old Kochi

Old Kochi is the peninsula comprising Fort Cochin and Mattancherri. Its has a long and fascinating history, and some of the most interesting buildings in India are to be found here – old Portuguese, Dutch and British architecture, preserved as a striking contrast to styles found in the rest of Kerala.

Most visitors first experience of Kochi is its waterfront, north of the main ferry station (turn right out of the alley that leads up from the water and it is about a 10-minute walk to a square overhung with large trees). Here are the famous **Chinese fishing nets**, a legacy of long years of trade with China. Other Chinese influences lie in the conical hats woven from palm leaves still sometimes worn by fishermen and the pagoda-like roofs of some traditional buildings.

The fishing nets, looking like large wooden spiders, are ingenious contraptions based on a cantilever. Finely balanced by a system of weights (usually large stones hung on ropes), they are lowered into the water and, after a suitable period, hauled up to trap fish in the bottom of the net. The catches are small and the nets cannot operate during the May–August monsoon when the sea is too rough, but it is a much more sustainable way of fishing than modern methods.

One of Kochi's Chinese fishing nets in action

St Francis's Church

Just behind the fishing nets, in the shady square, are lines of stalls selling fresh fish to the public (not all of it from the nets). Dotted around are small outdoor restaurants which will cook the fish you buy for a reasonable fee and serve it up with chips and cool drinks. Pleasant though this can be in the evening, make sure you bring plenty of mosquito repellent and cover up as much as possible.

Just inland from the nets and eateries, along Princess Street with its lovely examples of colonial architecture, is Kochi's main square. This open stretch of green is surrounded by lovely buildings, some discreetly expensive hotels and boutiques, and is overhung by large tamarind trees. The grass in the centre is used for cricket and football matches by local students. However, the main sight here is St Francis's Church.

Vasco da Gama's Church

St Francis's of Kochi (open Mon–Sat 7am–6pm) is the oldest European church in India, its change from Catholic church to Protestant shrine a reflection of Kochi's history. On Christmas Day, 1500, just two years after Vasco da Gama had landed near Kozhikode, the Portuguese were granted the right to trade on the Kochi coast. Three years later, Alphonso de Albuquerque built a stockade of coconut trunks lashed together with coir ropes on the site of today's Fort. There, in Fort St Emmanuel, five Franciscan friars built the chapel of St Bartholomew. After Admiral Almeida negotiated a more permanent settlement here in 1506, stone-and-mortar buildings were constructed, including the church of St Anthony, consecrated in 1516 on the site of the earlier chapel. Vasco da Gama, who had returned as the Governor of the Indies in 1524, died on Christmas Eve that same year during a visit to Kochi. He was buried in St Anthony's Church, and the original rails and tombstone still mark the location of his grave. Da Gama's remains were taken to Lisbon in 1538.

In 1663 St Anthony's passed into Dutch hands and became a Lutheran church, remaining so after Kochi came under British control in 1795. In the middle of the 19th century it became an Anglican church and acquired its present name, St Francis's. The church has several prized possessions, including a wealth of records such as a palm-leaf title deed which the local Raja gave to the Portuguese in 1503, and the Doop Boek, a Dutch baptismal register.

To the south of the square is **Santa Cruz Cathedral** (open Mon–Sat 9am–1pm, 3–5pm), Kochi's major Roman Catholic church. The original Portuguese-built Santa Cruz had been founded on a site to the north of its present location not long after the present-day St Francis's was consecrated. That building, which had been converted into an armoury by the Dutch, was

Kochi goats ingest some politicians

destroyed by the British in 1795 (an original pillar can be seen in the modern church), and it wasn't until 1903 that Santa Cruz was consecrated on its present site. The exceptionally colourful interior paintings are worth a look.

Mattancherri Palace

Turning left from the ferry jetty and walking down the long street lined with old spice merchants' buildings and warehouses (some of them still working) brings you to the district of Mattancherri, site of Kochi's two most fascinating monuments, the Mattancherri Palace and the Pardesi Synagogue.

The fascinating 16th-century **Mattancherri Palace** (open Sat–Thur 10am–5pm) was built by the Portuguese in 1555 and then given to the Raja of Kochi. Built in an amalgam of Portuguese Colonial and Keralan styles, it was extensively renovated by the Dutch in 1663, as a gift to Kochi royalty

Krishna reclining surrounded by the Gopis

(no doubt hoping to curry favour and gain better trade concessions), and so acquired its alternative name of the Dutch Palace.

The first room you enter is the Darbar Hall, in which the rajas of Kochi were crowned. Today it houses a series of royal portraits and gives an outline of the history of the royal family. To the

> The murals of Kerala are of a unique style which is known as 'Fresco-Seco'. They are painted with vegetable- and mineral-based colours, and then coated with pine resin. Various shades of ochre red, white, yellow and green are the predominant colours.

left you enter the Ramayana room and you see why the palace is so important. Covering the walls are wonderfully vibrant murals depicting the story of Rama and his battle with Ravanna. Look closely and you can also see the story of Krishna and the Gopis (female cowherds) interwoven with the epic. The room that leads off to the right from the Darbar Hall has portraits of the gods Vishnu, Siva and Parvati, Lakshmi and Rama and Sita.

More intriguing, however, is the rajas' bedchamber, reached by a steep wooden ladder. The first room you reach has preliminary sketches for further paintings, but the one beyond is decorated with erotic murals, including one of the seduction of Siva and Mohini discovered by Parvati in the background of which are mating animals, and a masterly depiction of a reclining Krishna surrounded by the Gopis.

Back upstairs, there are further rooms with displays of items associated with the royal household, including costumes and palanquins.

The same compound houses two temples used by the Kochi rajas, the Bhagavati Temple, and the circular Krishna Temple, which is a fine example of Keralan traditional temple design (neither are open to non-Hindus).

Jewish Kochi

Jewish trade with Kerala is thought to date back to Biblical times and certainly there would have been Jewish settlements after the Roman destruction of the Second Temple in Jerusalem in AD70, and records of AD370 speak of over 10,000 Jews living in and around Musiris, thought to be close to present-day Kodungallur.

Sephardic Jews came in the early 16th century when the Inquisition drove them from Spain and Portugal. They were joined by Ashkenazy Jews from Central Europe and they formed settlements separate from the existing Jewish population. That separation continued even when, fleeing Portuguese persecution in Kodungallur, the more recent immigrants came to Kochi.

The Pardesi Synagogue

There are very few Jews in Kochi today (most have emigrated to Israel, leaving around only some 11 members of the community to keep up the celebration of Jewish holidays), but the district has one or two streets where their presence can still be felt through their distinctive architecture and the ubiquitous presence of the Star of David.

The exquisite **Pardesi Synagogue** (open Sun–Fri 10am–noon, 3–5pm; closed on Jewish holidays) is the most visible symbol of this Jewish legacy. It was initially constructed in 1568 and rebuilt in 1664, two years after the Portuguese pogrom, and restored 100 years later. Hand-painted Chinese tiles, no two of which are the same, pave the floor, and the surprisingly light and airy interior hung with many glass lamps make the synagogue one of the most striking places of Jewish worship

Tiles from the synagogue's floor

anywhere. Its treasures include scrolls of law in the tabernacle, golden crowns given by the rajas of Travancore and Kochi, silver lamps presented by the first British Resident to the court of Kochi, and the two 10th-century copper plates from Bhaskara Ravi Varma that granted the Jews certain rights and privileges.

The Islands

The **Vembanad lagoon** that lies between Kochi and the mainland is dotted with islands. Some, such as Gundu, are very small and are barely inhabited. Vypeen, which lies opposite Kochi across the narrows by the fishing nets, is much larger. It stretches nearly as far as Kodungallur and at its far end are a pair of ruined Portuguese forts (one on the mainland, one on Vypeen itself) that protected the passage there.

To the south of Kochi is Bolghatty (the ferry from Ernakulam to Kochi passes very close to this as it rounds the point). This is chiefly known for its Dutch palace, built in 1744. Until 1947 it was the residence of the British Resident to the court of Kochi. The location of the palace is enchanting, but it was converted into a hotel and is now very run-down.

Spice warehouse workers, Kochi

South again, and across the main shipping channel leading into Kochi harbour, is Willingdon island. This is a man-made island, created in the early 20th century with sand dredged from the harbour, and is now the location of Kochi's port, the second busiest in India, and is highly industrialised, with shipyards, container depots and factories. It is also the headquarters of India's Southern Naval Command, and was previously the location of Kochi's airport (a new international terminal has been built 36km/22 miles north of the city).

Ernakulam

Across the harbour is the busy and expanding city of Ernakulam, a modern commercial centre. There are relatively few tourist sights here, but it is the location of the main railway station and M.G. Road is good for shopping. It also has a number of good hotels and can make a convenient, and cheaper, alternative base to Old Kochi. The Siva Temple, whose shrine can sometimes be seen appearing above the rooftops, is an important focal point for local Hindus, although non-Hindu visitors are not allowed in.

Close to the temple, which is just off M.G. Road, is Darbar Hall, on Darbar Hall Road. This impressive 19th-century building used to hold the Pariksith Thamburam Museum, but its exhibits have now been moved to the Hill Palace (*see below*). The building has been taken over by the **Kerala Lalit Kala Akademi** (Kerala Academy of Art), which uses it to hold temporary exhibitions of contemporary art. It has a fine collection of 19th-century paintings, copies of ancient murals and sculpture, and memorabilia from the Kochi royal family's collection.

The **Hill Palace Museum** (open Tues–Sun 9am–5pm) is in Tripunithura, about 10km (6 miles) southeast of Ernakulam. This building was the seat of the former ruling family of Kochi, and has now been converted into a museum. There is a fine collection of 19th-century paintings and memorabilia of the Kochi royal family on display.

Spices

The Phoenicians and the Greeks sailed to Kerala to gather spices. Indian pepper and cardamom were highly valued, and the ports of Musiris (now Kodungallur) and Ophir (present-day Beypore) are ancient ports of call. Arab sailors were also regular visitors to the Malabar Coast; they came to buy spices long before the advent of Islam, and the beaches of Kerala were busy entrepôts for the spice trade. Today the trade operates out of warehouses in Kochi.

Pepper was called black gold and was highly valued. Cardamom was another highly prized item and the small green fruit grows abundantly in the forests of the Cardamom Hills. India produces approximately 80 percent of the world's cardamom, and of this, 60 percent is grown in Kerala. Pepper has been the largest foreign exchange earner among India's cash crops, although the trade is now facing hard times and is under threat from cheaper spices grown in Vietnam. This has meant a crash in the world market and a rise in debt has seen a number of Keralan farmers (who produce around 40 percent of India's spices) commit suicide.

THE WESTERN GHATS

Kerala has South India's most impressive mountains, the Western Ghats, rising to a height of 2,695m (8,841ft) at the peak of Anaimudi. East of Kottayam lies plantation country: rolling estates of tea and coffee, rubber, cardamom and pepper, interspersed with forests and nature reserves. The Western Ghats north of the Periyar River are the High Ranges, locally called the Annamalais – the Elephant Hills – below the Periyar are the Cardamom Hills, not so high but thickly forested and developed only in their southernmost reaches.

Ponmudi and Neyyar

Ponmudi is Thiruvananthapuram's hill station. Located about 60km (35 miles) northeast of the capital, at a height of 1,066m (3,500ft) in the Cardamom Hills by the Tamil Nadu border, Ponmudi is cool and mist-shrouded almost all year round. Easily reached by bus, or as part of a tour, it provides a welcome escape during the heat of summer. It is surrounded by tea estates and forested hills, many of which offer fine treks.

Close by (10km/6 miles from Ponmudi) is the **Peppara Wildlife Sanctuary**. This has a good variety of plant and bird life, and a surprising number of butterflies.

The Western Ghats seen from Eravikulam

To get permission to trek off the beaten path you need to contact the Chief Wildlife Officer in Thiruvananthapuram (*see pages 25–35*).

Another beautiful spot is the **Neyyar Dam**, which is passed on the way up from Thiruvananthapuram. The dam itself has held back a large lake which was incorporated into a wildlife sanctuary in 1958. Although there are a fair number of species here, the more spectacular animals are rarely seen and the main activity seems to be boating on the lake.

Neyyar is also the location of the Sivananda Ashram, a well-run and peaceful yoga retreat that has attracted many Western visitors (see <www.sivananda.org> for details).

A waterfall on the road to Munnar

Peermade

North of Ponmudi, in Idukki District, surrounded by forests and meadowed hills is the artificial Periyar Lake. There is no direct road from the sights in the Cardamom Hills and visitors must travel up from Kottayam (a trip of around 120km/ 75 miles). The journey itself is part of the attraction as the road winds up the mountains, climbing through a carpet of tea bushes, estates of rubber trees and coffee, cardamom and pepper plantations. En-route it is possible to visit the waterfalls at Athirapalli (actually just inside Thrissur District). Set in the thick forests of the Sholayar Hills, the Chalakudi River plunges over a steep line of cliffs making a spectacular sight. There is accommodation close by and it can be a beautiful spot to hole up in for a couple of days.

A good place to rest during the journey onwards is the pretty little hill town of **Peermade**, about 75km (47 miles) from Kottayam. The settlement is a splash of colour surrounded by a carpet of tea estates, and set in rolling hills of dark green. Now well into the High Range, the road travels at heights of around 2,100m (7,000ft), which is about the height of the tallest peak in the Cardamom Hills, and there is a distinctly different feel to the air.

Thekkady

The road from Peermade joins the road from Madurai in Tamil Nadu at Kumili, and climbs to reach the villages of **Kumily** and **Thekkady**, which overlooks Periyar Lake. Buses from Kumily run up to Thekkady, which has a wide variety of accommodation and is the base and entry point for visiting the **Periyar Wildlife Sanctuary and Tiger Reserve** ◄ (open 6am–6pm), one of India's most successful wildlife protection projects. Covering an area of nearly 800 sq km (310 sq miles), at heights ranging from 900–1,950m (3,000–6,500ft), the surrounding forests were first put under a protection order by the Maharaja of Travancore in 1933 (the Maharaja's hunting lodge is now a hotel run by the KTDC), and the core area of 350 sq km (135 sq miles), to which there is no access, was declared a national park in 1982.

One of the most popular ways to see the sanctuary is to take a boat around the lake. Pleasant though this is, those more serious about spotting wildlife might want to go on a guided trek in a small group, lead by a forest ranger. The crowds on board the ferries tend to be excitable and noisy – not the best conditions for getting close to nervous animals.

This is one of the finest elephant sanctuaries in India,

> **Periyar has been one of India's more successful Project Tiger reserves, due in part to its policy of giving local forest communities partial access to the park so they can continue to carry out their traditional activities.**

Anaimudi, South India's highest peak

and herds of 20 to 30 elephants, sometimes more, are often spotted slowly meandering up and down the hillside, playing in the water or swimming across small necks in the lake to get to the other side.

Other species that inhabit the park include spotted deer and sambar, gaur and a variety of waterbirds that are easy to spot, although you need a great deal of luck and patience to see a bear, leopard or tiger, or birds of rare species. Nevertheless, given the beautiful surroundings, the experience can be wonderful however many animals you see.

Idukki

The road from Thekkady, along the line of the Ghats, leads on to Munnar, only about 70km (44 miles) away. However, its tortuous twisting and turning through the mountains makes it seem much further. On the way you pass through **Idukki**. Idukki means 'narrow gorge', and that is exactly what the Periyar River gushes through to the west of the Kumili–Munnar road.

On either side of the river, creating the gorge, are Kuravan and Kurathi, hills which, according to folklore, are Adivasi lovers who were turned into granite rocks because of a curse. Bridging the gorge is the Idukki arch dam, set against densely wooded hills and valleys traversed by hundreds of rushing streams. The dam is surrounded by forest, tea estates and the

Idukki Wildlife Sanctuary. While the flora and fauna in the sanctuary are similar to those in the Periyar sanctuary, it sees fewer visitors and has even fewer facilities.

Munnar

Heading towards **Munnar**, the road winds its way through endless tea plantations before arriving at the town. British companies owned most of the large plantations in Munnar, with the exception of one Indian, Kannan Devan. The most important planter in the High Range today is Tata Tea, which oversees almost every public facility in the vicinity.

Munnar is situated at the confluence of three rivers, at a height of about 1,800m (6,000ft). It is the highest town in Kerala and lies at the heart of tea country. It has some of the biggest tea estates in Kerala on either side of the High Range. Beyond, and visible from the town, lies Anaimudi

Colourful adverts in Munnar's bazaar

Picking tea in the Munnar fields

(the highest peak in the Western Ghats at 2,695m/8,842ft). Just outside Munnar, on the road to Tall Trees, is Sunset View Point. This high bluff overlooking the foothills and tea estates of the Ghats faces west and can be magical at sunset.

Munnar itself still maintains an air of the company town it once was. If commercial life still revolves around the tea industry, then the social life of the planters and managers of the estates still revolves around the High Range Club. Unfortunately, visits are only possible with an introduction from a member, so it is unlikely you will get to see the inside, still redolent of the British Raj.

Elsewhere in the town there is a small but lively bazaar and a colourful temple set on a hill. Many of the inhabitants are Tamils (the border with Tamil Nadu is very close) who have traditionally been contracted to work in the tea fields, and the language you are likely to hear is Tamil rather than Malayalam.

However pretty the surrounding tea estates might look, the work is extremely hard and although conditions have improved a little since Independence, the tea workers, the vast majority of whom are low-caste Tamil women, have faced a long history of exploitation and low wages.

Eravikulam National Park

Eravikulam National Park (open 7am–5pm) lies to the north of Munnar on the slopes of Anaimudi. Visitors are limited to a small section of the sanctuary near to the entrance to protect the rare flora and fauna of the region. The park was set up to protect the Nilgiri tahr, one of the rarest mountain goats in the world. Until a few years ago the species was fighting a losing battle for survival; now herds of 30 and more can be seen at any time. The tahr often come down to the main gateway where they seem unconcerned by the large numbers of visitors (it might be wise to avoid Sundays or public holidays when the park entrance becomes very crowded). The staggering views over the mountains and tea fields are one of the sanctuary's main attractions.

Mattupatty Lake and Top Station

A further excursion from Munnar is to the east, up to Mattupatty Lake and the viewpoint at Top Station (actually just

Tea and Coffee

Today India is the largest producer of tea in the world. Assam and Darjeeling lead the way, but much is grown in the south. The earliest tea plantations in South India were developed in the Nilgiri hills between 1859 and 1869. Tea in Kerala grows on the hill slopes of the Western Ghats and it is believed that the higher the elevation, the better the flavour. Tea plantations stretch all the way from the Nilgiri hills to the southern parts of Kerala. Most tea is prepared using the CTC method – crushing, tearing, curling – which produces a dark, strong brew.

Coffee arrived in India in the 17th century, nearly 200 years before tea. Hazarat Shahi Janab Allah Mogatabi, popularly known as Baba Budan, sowed seven coffee seeds he had brought from a pilgrimage to the holy places of Islam. The seeds were sown in the hills in Karnataka, which still bear his name. Kerala is the second-largest producer of coffee in India and during the coffee-blossom season, the plantations are decked with a mass of white flowers.

inside neighbouring Tamil Nadu). As you leave Munnar you might like to stop off at the Kerala Forest Development Corporation's **Orchidarium**, where there is a beautiful display of plants and flowers for sale.

The road on to Mattupatty winds up and up through beautiful landscape, dotted with tea estates, plantations and woods, all the while ringed by the mountains. The large **Mattupatty Dam** has created a large lake that extends back into the hills. You can hire boats to explore the waters further. About halfway along the lake you come to Echopoint (easily spotted by the hawkers that congregate here). Shouting out over the water, your words are bounced back from the opposite shore. On again, and much higher up, you reach Top Station, marked by a few tea stalls and basic eateries. The views from here are breathtaking, though they are sometimes obscured by mist.

The Munnar tea fields at sunset

THRISSUR AND GURUVAYUR

To the north of Ernakulam lie Thrissur and Palakkad districts. Here are some of the most important temples in all of Kerala, the Siva and Bhagavati temples at Kodungallur, the Vadakkunathan temple in Thrissur and the Guruvauyrappan temple in Guruvayur. Important places of worship are not restricted to the Hindu community, however, as there are also important mosques and churches across the region. Adding to the heterogeneous nature of the region, the Palakkad Gap, the lowest point in the Western Ghats, has for centuries been the main thoroughfare for peoples passing in and out of the Kerala region. Not surprisingly, there is a strong element of Tamil culture in the area around Palakkad. As the hills rise again to the north the forest become thicker and here is one of India's last areas of virgin rainforest, now protected as Silent Valley National Park.

> **The region to the north of Kochi is home to Kerala's most sacred shrines – at Guruvayur and Thrissur – and forms the Hindu heartland of the state.**

Kodungallur

Leaving Kochi by crossing over to Vypeen island and heading north, you pass a pair of Portuguese forts *(see page 51)* and then rejoin the mainland. Just beyond Azhikod is **Kodungallur**. Steeped in history, this settlement has been identified as the ancient port of Musiris, said to have been visited by the Romans, as well as being the site of India's earliest mosque.

The **Cheraman Mosque**, although it now has a modern appearance, is believed to be the oldest in India, its history predating the Mughal influence in the north and the Deccan. The architecture inside the modern facade points to the heavy influence of local Hindu design. It is said to have been

Festival worshippers at Kodungallur's Bhagavati Temple

founded by the Islamic missionary Malik ibn Dinar in 629. The present design dates from 2001 when it underwent a thorough restoration. The tombs of Malik ibn Dinar and his wife behind the main prayer hall are ecumenical, attended by both Muslim and Hindu women.

It was not only the Muslims who are first thought to have set foot in India on this spot. Kodungallur is also said to have been where the Apostle Thomas landed (in, allegedly, AD52). Close by, at Azhikod, the large church is said to hold the grizzly relic of St Thomas's forearm. The town was also one of the first places settled by Jews fleeing persecution.

There are, however, also very important Hindu shrines here. The **Tiruvanchikulam Temple** close to the mosque is a splendid Siva shrine, a fine example of traditional Keralan temple architecture, while the most lively and popular shrine in Kodungallur is undoubtedly the **Bhagavati Temple**, dedicated to the goddess, which sits in a large compound at the centre of the town. The Bhavani Festival in March–April, which involves drinking and the singing of sexually charged songs, held early in the year, sees many visitors. Both temples do not allow access to non-Hindus and visitors may wish to keep their distance at festival time.

Aluva and Parur

To the east of Kodungallur are the towns of Aluva and Parur (both reached more easily from Ernakulam). **Aluva** is now a busy industrial town on the banks of the Periyar River and is chiefly famous for its Sivaratri Festival. During this, the devotees pay homage to the Siva lingam on the sandbank and bathe in the river. Also on the riverbank is a splendid old palace. **Parur**, said to have been visited by St Thomas, was once a major Jewish settlement.

Kaladi and Malayattur

Close to Aluva, also on the banks of the Periyar River, is **Kaladi**. Now a rather drab town on a busy, and not very well-maintained, road, it was the birthplace of the great 8th-century Advaita philosopher and religious reformer Sankaracharya, and is still a major pilgrim centre. The shrine to the great philosopher has two temples: one contains an image of Sankaracharya as Daksinamurti; the other an image of Sarada, the deity of the *matt* (governing council of the temple) that maintains the shrine. Nearby is the modern, and striking, **Kirtistamba Mandapam**, a

Ritual ablutions at India's oldest mosque, Kodungallur

> However colourful and attractive the temple elephant parades may appear, the lives of the participating animals are less glamorous; they spend much of their time shackled by chains which often restrict their ability to stand or walk in comfort.

brick-built 46-m (150-ft), nine-tier octagonal tower, dedicated to Sankaracharya.

A few miles beyond Kaladi in **Malayattur**, at the top of a 610-m (2,000-ft) hill, is a shrine dedicated to St Thomas. The footprints in the rock are said to be those of the Apostle. The help of St Thomas, who is believed to have meditated here and built a shrine, is invoked every year by thousands of pilgrims. The festival here just after Easter sees one of the biggest Christian gatherings in South India.

To the west, near Kotamangalam on the Ernakulam–Munnar road, is the **Thattekkad Bird Sanctuary** (open 6am–5pm). The only bird sanctuary in Kerala, it encompasses both the Periyar River and teak plantations, an excellent setting for a large variety of birdlife including hornbills and parrots.

Thrissur

Thrissur (previously Trichur), one of the most sacred sites in Kerala, lies to the north of Kodungallur. The name Thrissur is an anglicised version of the Malayalam Trissivaperur, meaning 'Siva's town', and, at the centre of the town is the enormous **Vadakkunnathan Temple** (strictly closed to non-Hindus except during *Puram*; *see below*), dedicated to the god Siva. The temple is built on a round hill, surrounded by a public park and with gateways at each of the cardinal points. It is a typical example of Keralan temple architecture with pagoda-like roofs on the entranceways, and much exquisite woodcarving. Inside it contains shrines to Parvati, Sankaranarayana, Rama and Krishna, as well as the central shrine of Paramasiva. Legend has it that the temple was founded by the sage Parasurama, who established the land of Kerala *(see page 14)*. The Thrissur Temple celebrates its famous *Puram* festival every year in April. A spectacular affair, it involves a procession of 30–40 caparisoned elephants *(though see panel opposite)* amid the fanfare of the *panchavadyam,* a large trumpet, drum and cymbal ensemble comprising five different traditional Keralan musical instruments.

The city's **Archaeological Museum** (open Tues–Sun 10am–5pm) has recently been moved from the town centre to the Kollengode Palace, a 19th-century building about 2km (1 mile) from the city centre. It has an excellent collection of Megalithic finds from the surrounding area, some fine bronzes and interesting wooden models of different Keralan temples.

A gateway at the Vadakkunnathan Temple, Thrissur

Thrissur has a good claim to be the cultural capital of Kerala. Three state academies – the Kerala Sahitya Akademi (literature), the Sangeet Natak Akademi (music and drama) and the Lalit Kala Akademi (visual arts) – have their headquarters here. The School of Drama run by the University of Kozhikode is also based in Thrissur, and the Kalamandalam Art Academy *(below)* is not far off.

Kalamandalam lies about 30km (18 miles) from Thrissur on the Thrissur–Shoranur highway. This academy was founded by the Keralan poet, Vallathol Narayana Menon (1878–1958), in Cheruturuti on the banks of the Bharatapuzha River. The academy provides training in the dance forms *Mohiniattam, ottan tullal* and *Kathakali.* The latter was traditionally a male preserve but now some women are also trained in the style.

Devotees queuing to enter the Guruvayur Temple

Guruvayur

North of Thrissur, about 30km (18 miles) away, lies **Guruvayur** with its famous Krishna temple, considered the most sacred Hindu religious centre of Kerala. Though the origin of the temple is shrouded in mystery, there is no doubt that it existed from the 16th century at least. Legend says that the consecration of the temple was carried out by Guru,

the teacher of the *devas*
(gods), and Vayu, the god of
the winds, and so the place
came to be known as Guru-
vayur. Krishna, who is the
deity installed in the temple's
inner sanctum, is known as
Guruvayurappa.

Floral offerings at the temple

There are regular *pujas*
before dawn and at dusk
(when oil lamps are lit all
around the temple), which
attract thousands of devo-
tees (non-Hindus are not permitted within the temple and
guards strictly police the boundaries), and it is a particularly
auspicious place for Hindus to get married. At major festivals the queues for *darsan* (a view of the image of the god)
can be extremely long. The devotees give large donations in
cash and food, including grain, vegetables and *ghi*, and the
temple is one of the richest in the state.

The annual *Ulsavom,* or temple festival, at Guruvayur is
spread over 10 days in February–March, starting off with an
elephant race. There is also a colourful elephant procession
and a performance of *Krisnattam*, once particular to this
temple and the precursor of *Kathakali*. There is another festival in November–December when concerts by famous musicians are held at the temple.

Palakkad

Palakkad (formerly Palghat), at the base of the Western
Ghats, is a busy trading town set in a break in the hills, 79km
(49 miles) from Thrissur. It is the capital town of the district
which produces a great deal of Kerala's rice. It has a well-
preserved **fort** built by Hyder Ali in 1766, and used by his

A lotus blooms in a temple pool

famous son, Tippu Sultan, in his battles against the British. The fort is now maintained by the Archaeological Survey of India.

Fourteen kilometres (9 miles) from Palakkad is the Malampuzha Dam. The dam has been built across the Bharatapuzha River, near the foothills of the Western Ghats. The huge lake has an attractive terraced garden.

Palakkad is also the centre of *tolpavakuttu*, Kerala's shadow puppet plays. Across the district, close to the village temples, you may see small, two-storey buildings that are open on one side. These are the drama houses where the shadows of the puppets are projected onto a cloth as the story of Rama and Sita is sung. The version of the *Ramayana* that the puppeteers use is the Tamil Kamban version, which reached the area by trade through the Palakkad Gap.

Silent Valley

North of Palakkad is **Attappadi**, a centre of the Irular, Mudugar and Kurumbar peoples who traditionally dwelt in the thick forests of the Western Ghats. Twelve kilometres (7 miles) further on is **Silent Valley**, one of the few tropical evergreen rainforests left in the country. The biodiversity of the area is huge and, as a protected site, entry into the core area of the park is strictly regulated by the Forest Department with few people, save scientists, allowed to visit. However, the area around Silent Valley is beautiful, covered in forest and quiet plantations, perfect for exploring on foot and making the district well worth a visit.

NORTHERN KERALA

The northern part of the state is little explored by many visitors and as such has a much more off-the-beaten-track feel to it and you are less likely to encounter many other tourists. The coastal areas are the stronghold of Kerala's Muslim community, known as the Mapilas, a legacy of this coast's long history of trade with the Arabian Gulf. All along the coast are large mosques and extravagant 'Gulf' houses *(see page 12)*, many of them financed by migrant workers who flock to places such as Saudi Arabia and Dubai in search of employment. Life is hard for those who go, often to take up menial or labouring jobs with long hours and unsympathetic employers. Workers may not see their families for over two years but many still feel the sacrifice is worth it for the sums of money they earn: while often low in terms of the Gulf States, it is far above what many of them could earn in Kerala or elsewhere in India. This region is not without its historical significance either. Vasco da Gama first made landfall in India on this coast and the French enclave of Mahé is Malabar's answer to the Union Territory of Pondicherry (from which it is administered) on the east coast.

Ice cream on Kozhikode's beach

Kozhikode

► **Kozhikode** (previously called Calicut, a name which is still popular locally) is the major city of this part of Kerala. It was once the dominant port of the Malabar coast (a role now taken by Kochi), and known to the Phoenicians and the Greeks for its export of spices and cloth. The first colonial adventurer from the West, Vasco da Gama, landed near Kappad, 14km (8 miles) to the north. The Zamorin Raja welcomed him and allowed him the same trading rights as had been given to many other foreigners, but Portuguese ambitions made conflict inevitable and fierce sea battles were fought between the Portuguese and the Zamorin navy. The Portuguese were beaten back by the Zamorin's forces and were succeeded by the Dutch and later by the British, with a short French presence in between. The whole city was finally given over to the British in 1792.

The Misqalpalli mosque, Kozhikode

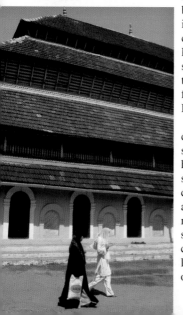

Kozhikode is a crowded commercial city, its streets spilling over with more than half a million people. It is still an important trading centre for spices, coconuts and other produce, and numerous lorries pull up on its sea front. At the centre of the city is the **Mananchira**, a large tank, or lake, built by one of the Zamorins to supply the city with water. During periods of severe water shortage it is still used by some of the city's people.

Kozhikode also has good connections with the rest of the state and further afield. Kozhikode has an international airport, chiefly with flights to the Gulf that are usually packed with migrant workers.

Mosques and Museums

The most interesting historical monuments can be found in the Kuttichira district. This is the old town of Kozhikode and home to many of the city's Muslims. Within the maze of narrow streets are the characteristic large mansions which would have been home to much of the extended family; many now, unfortunately, are falling into disrepair. Also here are two early and important sites, the **Misqalpalli and Machantipalli mosques**. The former dates back to the 14th century, despite its present 16th-century appearance; it was reconstructed following canon damage by the Portuguese captain Albuquerque in 1510. The lands for the Machantipalli mosque were granted in the 13th century. Both are fascinating in their adherence to local traditional forms of architecture, with stepped roofs and delicate woodcarving.

> **The name of Calicut (an English mispronunciation of the difficult Malayalam spelling) lent itself to the English word calico. This is a type of cotton fabric that was originally exported from here.**

As befits a trading centre the city also once had, like Mumbai, a thriving Parsi community. There is still a fire temple on S.M. Street but, like the Jewish community of Kochi, there are very few members now left.

In the east of the city, both within the same shady compound on top of a small hill, are two museums. The interesting **Pazhassiraja Museum** (open Tues–Sun 10am–1pm,

Catching up on the train to Kozhikode

2–4.30pm) is managed by the State Archaeological Survey. Pazhassi Raja was a local ruler who led an uprising against the British at the end of the 18th century. The museum has a good collection of local 17th- and 18th-century bronzes, as well as an extensive sculpture gallery (downstairs). There are one or two good models showing the design of traditional Keralan temples and, most bizarrely, a collection of Raj-era hats from the Travancore Excise Department.

Beside the museum is the **Art Gallery and Krishna Menon Museum** (open Thur–Sat 10am–5pm, Wed 1–5pm). The Art Gallery is currently closed for maintenance, while the other section is dedicated to displays on the life of the prominent post-Independence politician who was India's representative to the United Nations during the 1950s.

Just to the south of Kozhikode lies the major fishing harbour of **Beypore** at the mouth of the River Chaliyar. Once known to Roman and Arab traders, Beypore is being revived as a port. It has a boat-building yard which has been making vessels for peoples from the Gulf and Kuwait for centuries.

Wayanad

Fifty-five kilometres (34 miles) east of Kozhikode is the **Wayanad plateau**, 610m (2,000ft) high. Wayanad is known for its plantations of coffee, cardamom, pepper and rubber. There are also extensive tracts of unspoilt forest here, providing one of the great draws for visitors. For those with the money, a stay at the eco-resort at **Vythiri** *(see page 137)*, set in deep forest, is fabulous.

Wayanad is a separate district with headquarters at **Kalapetta**. There is a famous Jain temple here (Kalapetta was once the stronghold of the Jains), and caves in nearby **Edakkal** with prehistoric engravings of animals. One of the caves now contains a small restaurant. The town of **Sultanbathery** is chiefly famous for its now very ruined fort built by Tippu Sultan, from which it gets its name.

Between Vythiri and Kalapetta is the small settlement of **Laikidi** and the lake at **Pukote**. Both are set in spectacular countryside and the views from Laikidi (700m/2,296ft) in particular are wonderful. Overlooking both of these is **Chembra Peak**, the highest point in the district at 2,100m (6,890ft). Tour operators in the region can arrange treks to its summit.

Of great importance is the **Wayanad Wildlife Sanctuary** at **Muthanga** (18km/11 miles east of Sulthanbathery; open 6–8am, 3–5.30pm).

Wild flowers proliferate in the hills

> **The northern coastal districts of Kerala are a Mappila, or Muslim, stronghold. Lining the roads are numerous mosques as well as some of the state's most outrageous examples of Gulf architecture** (see page 12).

This vast swathe of forest is joined to the Mudumalai and Bandipur sanctuaries in Tamil Nadu and Karnataka respectively, making it part of the Nilgiri Biosphere. Home to many species of animal, bird and plant life, it is part of one of the largest and most important protected areas in India.

Kappad and Mahé

To the north of Kozhikode the highway passes through the suburb of West Hill to **Kappad** beach 15km (9 miles) away. Said to be where Vasco da Gama landed, it is now a quiet village with an attractive seashore. The spot where he landed is marked by a stone obelisk, set just inland near the road junction at the southern end of the beach. The beach itself is not very clean though you might be able to swim off the beach near the KTDC hotel above the northern headland.

Further up the coast you pass the quiet town of **Quilandy**. Due to the prevailing sea conditions it is thought that nearby Kollam (see pages 37–8) is a more likely spot for Vasco da Gama's first landing than Kappad. All around here is evidence of Arab trading and settlement and some families can trace their descent from Arab settlers.

Northward from Quilandy you reach **Mahé**, formerly a French enclave and now administratively part of Pondicherry. It still maintains a French air through its town planning and it retains a number of colonial buildings, including the baroque church of St Therese and the former French residency. The now ruined fort provides good views, but aside from these life mostly revolves around the beachfront.

Thalasseri and Kannur

About 5km (3 miles) from Mahé is **Thalasseri** (formerly Tellicherry). The **fort** was built by the East India Company in the early 18th century overlooking the Arabian Sea (open 10am–5pm). The small State Arts Museum here has excellent bronzes and woodcarvings. Close to the fort the **Odotilpalli Mosque**, similar in style to the Misqalpalli Mosque in Kozhikode, dates from the 17th century.

Thalasseri is well known for its Circus Academy and Gymnasium, built near the beach. Most Indian circuses are now full of gymnasts trained in the Thalasseri academy.

Close to Thalasseri, at Tiruvangad, is **C.V.N. Kalari**, founded by C.V.N. Nair back in the 1920s. It was set up to train artists in *kalaripayattu*, the Keralan martial art. With the aid of sticks and staves and the thin steel swords known as *urumi*, the fighters demonstrate superb gymnastic skill.

Fishing boats pulled up on the beach

Fishing off the rocks at Bekal Fort

Northwards, 29km (18 miles) away, lies **Kannur** (formerly Cannanore), once the capital of the Kolathiri Rajas and also the seat of the Arakkal Ali Rajas, the only Muslim ruling family in Kerala. **St Angelo's Fort** (open 8.30am–5.30pm), built by the Portuguese in the 16th century, gives fantastic views over the interesting Muslim town below. Close to the fort is the ancestral home of the Arakkal Ali Rajas (closed for renovation at present).

From Kannur to the border beyond Kasaragode *(see below)* is the heartland of *Teyyam*. This fascinating and colourful possession-dance is one of the cultural treasures of the state. The dances, in which a lavishly costumed male dancer is possessed by a powerful female deity such as Bhagavati or Chamundi, are performed at local festivals and paid for by a local family. The dances can be hard to track down as they are often performed at small village shrines and are not publicised (this is an act of worship not entertainment). However, your local host might be able to help you track them down. Note that women are not allowed in the shrine's compound, but are welcome to observe from outside.

Kasaragode and Bekal

About 100km (63 miles) north of Kannur on the National Highway lies the fishing centre of **Kasaragode**, which is just before the border with neighbouring Karnataka which lies across the Netravati River. The Muslims of the town are considered expert seamen. The wonderful beach here, on which they pull up their boats, stretches as far as Bekal, some 10km (6 miles) to the south. Note, however, that local coastal communities are not used to people swimming or sunbathing and might take offence, and many of the beaches are used as toilets.

Between Kannur and Kasaragode lie the little-known **Valiaparamba Backwaters**. Similar to those of southern Kerala, they are fringed by mangroves in places making them a wonderful place for bird-watching. They are slowly being discovered by local tour operators and it is now possible to hire boats for cruises.

Situated on a jutting beachhead high above the shore, at a strategic curve on the coast, is **Bekal Fort** (open 8am–5pm). Built of red laterite by the Nayaks in the 16th century, it eventually fell into the hands of Haider Ali. It was one of Tippu Sultan's most important fortifications and it passed to the British on his defeat in 1799.

A *Teyyam* dancer

LAKSHADWEEP

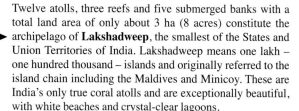

Twelve atolls, three reefs and five submerged banks with a total land area of only about 3 ha (8 acres) constitute the archipelago of **Lakshadweep**, the smallest of the States and Union Territories of India. Lakshadweep means one lakh – one hundred thousand – islands and originally referred to the island chain including the Maldives and Minicoy. These are India's only true coral atolls and are exceptionally beautiful, with white beaches and crystal-clear lagoons.

Until 1956, the islands formed part of the state of Madras, and were known until 1973 as the Laccadive, Minicoy and Amindivi Islands. Only ten of the islands are inhabited. They are, in descending order of size, Minicoy, Andrott, Kavaratti, Kadmat, Agatti, Kalpeni, Amini, Kiltan, Chetlat and Bitra. However, entry to many of the islands is restricted to protect the fragile ecosystem, which consists of lagoons and land which is barely 2m (6ft) above sea level.

The population of Lakshadweep is relatively high, just over 60,000 in 2001. Most of the islanders are of Keralan descent – originally Hindu, as the prevalent systems of caste and of matrilineal inheritance bear out. The language spoken on all the islands except Minicoy is a dialect of Malayalam. Mahl is normally spoken in Minicoy, which is close to and has historical links with the Maldive group of islands. Ninety-six percent of Minicoy's population is Muslim, Islam having been brought to the islands by Hazrat Ubaidullah in the 7th century.

Access to the islands is controlled and limited by

> **International tourists are permitted to stay only at Bangaram and Kadmat, both of which were originally uninhabited; Indian nationals, however, can stop over at Agatti, Kalpeni, Minicoy and the capital, Kavaratti.**

Idyllic beaches and clear, tropical lagoons

the Indian Government, and foreign tourists must book through one of two tour operators. For **Bangaram Island Resort**, contact CGH Earth (<www.cghearth.com>), for **Kadmat**, contact Lacadives (<www.lacadives.com>). Both operators offer diving packages for experts as well as beginners. If you are planning on diving you will need a certificate of health from your doctor. It may, at times, be possible for foreign tourists to stay at the small resort complex close to the airport on Agatti.

The only accommodation available on the islands is sparsely furnished tourist huts, though the bungalows on Agatti are more comfortable. Aside from flying from Kochi to Agatti (the only island with an airport) from where you transit by boat, there is a fleet of ships that make regular sailings from Kochi (see <www.lakshadweep.nic.in> for details of tours and the latest timetables) and provide accommodation on-board for the passengers.

WHAT TO DO

SPORTS

While Kerala is as cricket-mad as the rest of India, it is unusual in also having a strong following for its football teams (something it has in common with that other bastion of India's communists, West Bengal). The stadiums and players may not have the glamour and skills of those in South America or Europe but matches can still excite local passions and football pitches can be found in most major towns. That said, there is little other scope for attending spectator sports in the state. There are none of the large test-match cricket grounds found elsewhere in India and, apart from the traditional art of *kalaripapayattu* *(see page 77)*, few other obvious sporting events. Participant sporting activities, meanwhile, tend to centre on the long, palm-fringed Malabar coast.

The Malabar coast is lined with inviting beaches. However, the currents along the coast are very dangerous and strong and there are a number of drownings every year. Be very careful when swimming.

Water Sports

The two main tourist beaches in Kerala are **Kovalam** and **Varkala**, both close to Thiruvananthapuram. While both offer good swimming and reasonably alert lifeguards *(see the warning in panel above)* they still have little in terms of the organised activities you find elsewhere in the world, such as diving or parascending. A few of the local fishermen will, for a reasonable price, take you out in one of their traditional boats for an hour or so.

Although there are wonderful-looking beaches all along the
Keralan coast, not many of them are suitable for swimming or
sunbathing. The beaches are both a place for work and a toilet
for many coastal villages, which makes them unsuitable for
frolicking. Also traditional, often Muslim, communities would
be shocked by half-naked visitors appearing on their beach.

Instead of being in the water another option is to be on it.
One alternative is to go on a *kettuvallam* cruise *(see below)*.
Make sure you book through a reputable operator such as
Tour India (<www.tourindiakerala.com>). For the lesser-
known northern backwaters *(see page 79)* contact **Bekal
Boat Stay** (<www.bekalboatstay.com>). Additionally there
are a number of places where you can hire rowing boats,
such as Akkulam Boat Club (open 10am–5pm) or Veli

Kettuvallam Cruises

Kettuvallam are the boats historically used for transporting rice and
coir around the Backwaters. Their name derives from the Malayalam
for 'tied' and traditionally they were made of slotted planks tied
together (however, the planks on modern boats are nailed as the vibr-
ration from internal engines makes ropes work loose). With the rise of
other forms of transport the boats started to disappear from the lakes
and canals until, around 25 years ago, someone had the idea of using
them for tourist cruises.

Now there are about 400 boats plying the Backwaters, the characteristic hooped thatch housing bedrooms and a kitchen. Tours take
between one and five days, and you eat and sleep on the boat. This
can be an idyllic experience, watching everyday life on the banks and
seeing the palm trees glide by. However, cheaper boats may have
poor facilities and little shaded space outside (essential in the strong
midday sun). It is also important that the boat has a biotoilet – a
closed system that does not release sewage into the waters.

A *kettuvallam* prepares to set sail

Tourist Village (open 10am–5pm), both near Thiruvanantha-puram, or on Neyyar Dam *(see page 55)* and Pukote *(see page 75)* up in the Western Ghats.

However, the best watersports facilities are undoubtedly to be found in Lakshadweep *(see pages 80–1)*, where the swimming, snorkelling and diving are all superb. It is also possible to hire small sailing boats and canoes with which to explore the lagoons.

Wildlife and Trekking

Flanked to the west by the Arabian Sea and along the east by the Western Ghats, Kerala is well endowed with dense vege-tation supporting a rich and varied fauna. Forest still covers around 24 percent of the state and nearly 6 percent of that is protected. There are a number of excellent national parks and sanctuaries with ample opportunities for spotting species such as gaur, elephant and, occasionally, tiger. The bird-

A Nilgiri tahr

watching can also be immensely rewarding. For details regarding access and facilities (such as guided walks with forest guards or hides) contact: The Chief Wildlife Warden, Forest Headquarters, Vazhuthacaud, Thiruvananthapuram 695 014; tel: (0471) 252 9241; fax: 233 8806. Information about the individual parks and sanctuaries can also be found on <www.keralaforest.org>. Some of the most rewarding parks and sanctuaries in the state are listed below:

Eravikulam National Park Established to protect the highly endangered Nilgiri tahr and easily accessible from Munnar *(see pages 60–1)*.

Idukki Wildlife Sanctuary Near Idukki Dam *(see page 59)*.

Neyyar Sanctuary Wet tropical evergreen forest around the Neyyar Dam *(see page 55)*.

Peppara Sanctuary A small area of the Western Ghats near Vithura with fascinating bird life *(see pages 54–5)*.

Periyar Wildlife Sanctuary and Tiger Reserve The jewel in the crown of Kerala's national parks with a large population of elephants *(see page 57)*.

Silent Valley National Park Primary tropical rainforest with very restricted access *(see pages 63 and 70)*.

Thattekkad Bird Sanctuary Superb bird-watching on the Periyar River *(see page 66)*.

Wayanad Wildlife Sanctuary An immensely important forested reserve high in the Western Ghats *(see pages 75–6)*.

With such spectacular scenery in the Western Ghats Kerala has, potentially, some of the best trekking anywhere in

India outside of the Himalayas. While it is still relatively a low-key activity, trekking is becoming more popular and is offered by a number of tour operators. Palakkad District has some superb walks, as does the area around Munnar. The Periyar Tiger Trail is a particularly rewarding trek (contact <www.tourindiakerala.com> for details). To find reputable tour operators who should adhere to a strict ecological code of conduct contact the Adventure Tour Operators Association of India (<www.indiaadventure.com>).

ENTERTAINMENT

Kerala does not have a nightlife comparable to that of Mumbai, Chennai or Goa and, with the exception of the cities, much of the state shuts down after dusk, even if Keralans are said to drink the most of any Indian state. The resorts of Kovalam and Varkala have a laid-back nightlife revolving around the cafés and restaurants along the cliffs and seafront.

A *Kathakali* dancer

Kochi has some lovely restaurants that make for a pleasant night out *(see page 138)*, while Ernakulam on the mainland has **Loungevity** at the Avenue Regent on M.G. Road. This chic cocktail bar is Kerala's first 'designer' bar, all glass and marble (open 7pm–late, women's night Wed).

Kathakali

One very popular activity for visitors, however, is to attend a *Kathakali* performance. This spectacular dance-drama is famous for its elaborate make-up and heavy costumes *(see pages 12–13)*. While you would be lucky to catch a performance in its traditional venue beside a temple, a number of companies put on versions for tourists. Most places will allow you to arrive early so you can see the actors applying their make-up, an art in itself.

The centre for these performances is Fort Kochi, and two reputable companies are: the **Cochin Cultural Centre** (Carvetty Road, Fort Kochi; daily performances starting at 6.30pm); and the **Kerala Kathakali Centre** (off River Road, Fort Kochi; daily performances, make-up from 5pm, dance 6.30–8pm; <www.kathakalicentre.com>). Both places also run short courses in Keralan dance and music.

An *Ayurvedic* massage

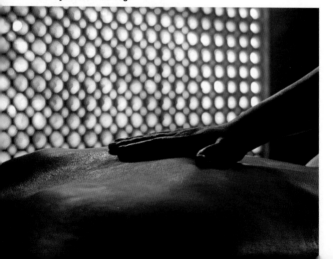

AYURVEDA

The traditional Indian system of healing known as *Ayurveda* is said to be based on the teachings contained in the *Vedas* (Hindu holy scriptures). Using a combination of herbs, oils, massage and meditation, often over a series of days or weeks, its practitioners

It is no coincidence that *Ayurveda* became established so strongly in Kerala. The extraordinary biodiversity of Kerala's flora means that there are a huge number of potentially healing plants from which *Ayurvedic* practitioners can derive their treatments.

claim to heal and put the elements of the body back into balance. It is a highly complex system and anyone contemplating treatment for a serious condition is urged strongly that they get professional advice before embarking on a course of treatment.

However, many visitors undergo shorter treatments which often amount to no more than a pleasant massage with scented oils, or herbal face packs, while lying on a wooden bench. This has been a boom area in Keralan tourism in recent years and you will be hard pressed to find a resort that does not offer at least some form of *Ayurvedic* massage or beauty treatment.

The most common treatments are as follows:

Dhara similar to *Sirovasti*

Kizhi warm bags containing herbs laid on the body

Pizhichil cloth soaked in medicated oils laid over the body

Sirovasti medicated oils dripped on your forehead

Sukhatirummu a massage with oils.

These treatments can be used in combinations and in addition you may be asked to eat some herbs *(Snehpanam)* as opposed to having heated bundles of herbs laid on your body *(Svedam)* to help you perspire.

SHOPPING

As with elsewhere in India, there is a large variety of local crafts, fabrics, food, books and jewellery to tempt the visitor into spending money. Specifically Keralan items might be harder for the foreign visitor to pick out from the range of goods found in the average tourist shop. It is much better to head for either government-run emporia, or locally owned shops away from the main tourist areas (look for where the locals shop as a good guide for where to go). The state government emporium is known as **Kairali**, with branches in Ernakulam (on M.G. Road), Kozhikode (on M.M. Ali Road) and Thiruvananthapuram, where it is called the SMSM **Handicrafts Emporium** (just behind the Secretariat building).

One of Kerala's exports is items made from coir (coconut fibre). This is spun and made into all kinds of mats, carpets and bags, often at a very reasonable price but sometimes not very transportable (though bulkier items can be posted quite easily; parcels must be sewn into cloth-covered bags by a local tailor before they are posted). Alappuzha is the centre of the coir industry and is probably the best place to look.

Fabrics of all kinds have long been a speciality of India, and the range of fibres and colours can be overwhelming. Shopping for fabric is one of the great pleasures of India, with bales of cloth thrown in front of you from which to make your choice. Silks are one of the best buys, though India produces some extremely fine cottons. *Khadi* fabrics are both handspun and handwoven by local artisans and can be some of the most characterful textiles. A speciality of Kerala is the traditional white blouse and skirt or sari, known as *mundu*, with a gold border *(zari)*.

All towns have their fabric shops. In Thiruvananthapuram try **Partha's** on Powerhouse Road (they also have a branch in Ernakulam on M.G. Road), which has a huge selection of

Saris for sale at Partha's, Thiruvananthapuram

dress fabrics and ready-made clothes, or **Alapatt Silks** in East Fort. In Kochi a lovely modern shop selling designer clothes and items for the home is **Cinnamon** (Ridsdale Road, by the Parade Ground; tel: 0484-221 7124).

Traditional gold jewellery can be exquisite, with delicate interwoven strands and characteristic small bobbles. It is generally sold by weight, and the day's gold price should be displayed in the shop. Don't expect jewellery to be cheap, especially if gems are included in the piece. Do make sure, as well, that you buy from a reputable jeweller. One of the largest chains in the state is **Alukkas**. They have branches in Thiruvananthapuram (East Fort), Ernakulam (M.G. Road), Alapuzzha (Boat Jetty Road) and Thrissur (Round East, by the temple). Another very reputable chain is **Josco**. They can be found in Thiruvananthapuram (East Fort), Kottayam (K.K. Road), Ernakulam (M.G. Road), Thrissur (M.O. Road) and Palakkad (G.B. Road).

Centa **drummers at a festival**

Other items worth looking out for include brass temple lamps and woodcarvings (both are Keralan specialities). Although the rules for exporting antiques from India are very strict, you can find some very fine items (all passed for export) at **Natesans** on M.G. Road in Thiruvananthapuram.

CHILDREN

Perhaps contrary to general perception, India is an easy country in which to travel with children. Indians love children and are very tolerant and indulgent with them, and children will find the sights and sounds of the country just as rewarding as adults.

However, there are some things you might want to bear in mind. Children can be more easily affected by the heat, unsafe drinking water and unfamiliar food seasoned with chillies and spices. Keep them covered up and use a very high factor sun cream. There are many varieties of bottled drinks and some foods, such as bananas and 'veg puffs', are innocuous, safe and widely available. In case of diarrhoea, rehydration salts are vital. Keep children away from wild and stray animals, especially dogs and monkeys. To avoid the risk of rabies, it may be safer to give children an anti-rabies vaccine.

For infants, it can be difficult to find nappies and places to change them. Consider bringing a supply of disposables, or changing to terries which, after rinsing, can be given to the hotel laundry. For touring, walking and hiking, a child-carrier backpack is well worth considering.

Calendar of Events

Pongal This harvest festival – generally only seen in the Tamil areas of the Western Ghats such as Munnar – occurs in January. Houses are cleaned and bonfires made of all that's not needed; rice – with milk and jaggery – is cooked in the open on open hearths and the resulting *pongal* is offered to the gods; cows are decorated and worshipped.

Palace Music Festival 6–12 January, annual festival in honour of Svati Tirunal with concerts of *Karnatak* music.

Malabar Mahotsavam 13–16 January, an annual celebration of the Keralan performing arts, held in Kozhikode.

Republic Day 26 January, celebrates the establishment of the Indian Republic with parades.

Malayattoor Festival In Malayattoor during March/April; hilltop celebrations and fulfilment of vows at the shrine of St Thomas.

Puram This major event in Thrissur in April/May has a parade of over a 100 decorated bull elephants *(see page 67)*. Also part of the festivities are dancers and musicians playing in the traditional *Pancavadyam* and *Centa Melam* ensembles.

Independence Day 15 August, the commemoration of India's independence from the British, celebrated with parades.

Onam This is Kerala's harvest festival in August/September. Floral and earth decorations are made and there are snake-boat races in Alappuzha, Kochi, Payipad and Aranumula. Traditional dances, music recitals and cultural shows also accompany this festival.

Navaratri (Nine Nights) The highlight of these 10 days and 9 nights in September/October is the music festival in Thiruvananthapuram, and the ritual procession down to the beach at Sanmukham.

Sabrimala Festival November–January, the pilgrimage season for devotees to worship at the Sabrimala temple *(see panel on page 42)*.

Christmas and New Year The Syrian Christian celebrations are quite low-key. No presents are given and Hindu influences are evident in the fireworks, torch-lit processions, nativity plays and singing which goes on until early in the morning. The Kochi Carnival takes place at New Year.

EATING OUT

Food in Kerala is likely to be a revelation to the first-time visitor. There is a huge variety, which is perhaps to be expected given the diversity of Kerala's population, and the tastes are often fresh and exciting. The cooking of Kerala is very different from that of the rest of India (though the South and North India staples of *dosa*, *idli* and *tanduri* dishes are easily found here), with coconut, bananas and tapioca forming a large part of the diet.

> Some of the best, and cheapest, places to eat are local 'meals' restaurants. They are usually very clean and have a quick turnover of food. You will be served a huge mound of rice surrounded by a variety of curried vegetables, pickles, curd and often some sweet *payasam*.

Keralan food is basically vegetarian; rice, the basic staple, is accompanied by various vegetable preparations and an array of curries – dishes with sauces that are used to mix with the rice. Non-vegetarians usually add only a mutton, chicken or fish dish to this spread. Beef is generally cooked only in Christian and Muslim homes and pork only in Christian homes.

Meals revolve around rice, eaten with *dal*-based soups, thin and spicy *rasams* and the thicker *sambars*, often flavoured with tamarind. To these are added 'sambar powder', made up of spices such as coriander, fenugreek seeds, cumin and the pungent spice asafoetida. Often they are finished by 'tempering': chillies and whole spices heated in oil until the important black mustard seeds pop; the whole lot is then poured on the top of the dish. Dry vegetable dishes and in certain places spicy meat and fish preparations are also served with the rice, to which is added copious quantities of curd (yoghurt) and fiery pickles.

Rice and Chips

In Kerala parboiled rice is generally used. This distinctive fat-grained rice, flecked with pink, is made by partially boiling the raw rice in its husk. The rice is then left to cool and the husk removed. The rice is cooked is the normal fashion but, unlike other types, it retains all its vitamins. Parboiled rice has been credited with the absence of rickets from Kerala due to its high levels of vitamin D.

Bananas, both raw and ripe, are used in various types of curries and as crisps in Keralan cooking. The banana 'chips' made in Kozhikode are famous, the wafer-thin round slices are dropped into very hot coconut oil. Boiled bananas are a popular dish for breakfast in some regions, while slices of banana dipped in batter and deep fried (again preferably in the hugely fattening coconut oil) are extremely tasty as a mid-afternoon snack.

Serving coffee in the Indian Coffee House, Thiruvananthapuram

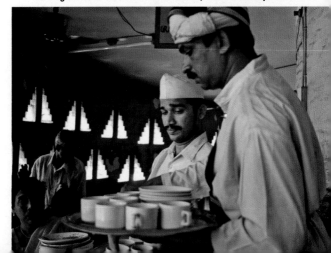

Pappadams, big and small, made with various combinations of ground grain but without masala (spices), and fried in oil, are often supplied as part of a meal.

Other Keralan specialities you might get with your meal include *olan* (a thin curry made of pumpkin and coconut) and *kalan* (made of gourd with yoghurt and coconut). Among some of the other delicious vegetable dishes are *kutus*, thick curries of various ingredients, and *avial*, a light vegetable curry in a coconut sauce. The Keralan *kadumanga* pickle – tender mangoes mixed with powdered chillies and mustard – is tasty and mild. At festival time you may also be served *pongal* and *uppuma* (made of rice or semolina mixed with spices).

Avial and *appam*

You may also come across vegetables with which you are not familiar. A common one is the drumstick, a long, woody vegetable which comes from a tree (you are not expected to eat the fibre but to suck the fleshy part off of it). *Kappa* is tapioca root, sometimes used boiled as an alternative to rice.

Breads and Appams

Although they are not specifically Keralan, you will find *chapatis* and *puris* available, either for breakfast with a potato *masala*, or as tiffin (a light meal). You will also come across the pan-South India favourites such as *dosas* (pancakes made of rice and lentils), *idlis* (steamed rice cakes) and *vadas* (fried doughnuts made of lentils), all of which can make a good breakfast.

Parottas are a Keralan speciality and a real treat. You will see these fat coils of dough impregnated with oil or *ghi* ready to be cooked on many roadside stalls. They are flattened and then grilled to make a delicious bread.

Snacks on the railway

An *appam*, a true speciality of Kerala, is made of ground rice and coconut with no oil used in the cooking. It is eaten with coconut milk or with any vegetarian or non-vegetarian curry. The steamed *idiappam* is made of rice flour and looks like vermicelli (similar to the 'string hoppers' you find in Sri Lanka). The *vellappam* and the slightly heavier *kallappam* are akin to *dosas*. *Puttu* are little round columns of steamed ground rice and coconut. All are very popular as breakfast dishes.

Snacks

Keralans are very fond, like most Indians, of snacking and you will come across a variety of deep-fried savouries in various shapes and sizes, ranging from the concentric *murukkus* to *omapodis* and savoury *bundis*. You will also see crispy, deep-fried coiled *appams*. All these snacks are made of rice and gram flour, and fried in oil. *Bhajis* and *pakoras*, vegetable or onion fritters dipped in a batter of ground gram flour, are also very popular. *Vadas*, served hot or cold, are also widely available *(see above)*.

Non-Vegetarian Dishes

Although much of the food you will see is vegetarian, Keralans, particularly from the Christian and Muslim communities, do eat a lot of meat and fish (usually prepared with the ubiquitous coconut). Seafood is plentiful due to the state's long coastline and a typical non-vegetarian meal consists of rice and fish curry. Fish is cooked in a variety of ways, including, fish *moilli* (a basic fish curry), *min varattiyathu* (fish in a thick *masala* sauce), *masala* fried fish, *min mulagittathu* (fish in a thin sauce made of chillies and tamarind or raw mangoes) and *min vattichathu* (fish in a thick coconut sauce with tamarind and a little chilli).

A dish eaten by Christians from Central Kerala is the delicious *min pollichatu* (a kind of baked fish curry). A local va-

---

Local Drinks

As well as soft drinks and beer, Kerala has a number of traditional drinks. Tea and coffee are available everywhere. Tea is served milky and sweet whereas coffee, unlike elsewhere in India, is often served black and can be extremely good. Buttermilk is widely available and is not only good at cooling your mouth from hot food, but is surprisingly refreshing in the heat. Keralan alcoholic drinks are toddy and arrak. The palm-wine toddy *(kallu)* is produced from the sap of the coconut palm. Toddy is also made from the increasingly rare pana tree, which produces the very tasty *pana kallu*. Toddy tappers climb the palms and attach an earthenware pot over the cut stem of a frond into which the sap drains. The quick-fermenting and brackish toddy tastes best early in the morning fresh from the palm tree. By lunch it may well have developed a sweet, slightly rancid flavour. Toddy is sometimes distilled into arrak, but this spirit is usually made from sugar-cane molasses. Arrak is probably best avoided as much of it comes from illicit stills and the results can be highly toxic.

riety of tamarind called *ko-dampuli* or *minpuli* is said to have medicinal qualities and is popular in central Travancore. It gives the 'Christian' style of these fish-based dishes their particular taste. The most popular fish is the *karimin*, the pearlspot which lives in brackish water.

Tapping for toddy

Traditionally a food of the poor, tapioca and fish, boiled together with turmeric and chillies, is both filling and nourishing (and often fiery hot). The steamed rice cakes, *puttu*, are a popular breakfast item, both eaten with boiled gram in *masala* or with fish.

Muslims, especially in the northern Malabar area, cook a variety of delicious, often non-vegetarian, dishes. Rice chapatis, called *pathiri*, are served with a variety of chicken and lamb dishes. Stuffed chicken, stuffed fish, *min pathiri* (steamed rice with a fish *masala*) and mussels stuffed in their shells, steamed and later fried, are some of the other dishes worth trying. The Mappila version of *biryani*, *naichoru*, is delicious, made with chicken, lamb or occasionally beef.

Sweets and Fruit

The common sweet after a meal, particularly on special occasions, is *payasam*, a liquid milk-based pudding with either rice or vermicelli, and a little aromatic spice for flavour. Kerala also has *ada prathaman,* which is also milk-based, and the *chakka prathaman* made of ripe jackfruit and *gur* (jaggery). Boiled ripe banana or candied banana chips go with the meal. Sweets commonly seen all over India are also seen in Kerala: the spherical *laddu*, made of gram flour and sugar; the *jalebi* and *jangri*, made of fermented flour or lentils, deep fried in circular patterns and soaked in sugar syrup; *gulab jamuns* made of dried milk and drenched in syrup; and a variety of *halvas*.

If your visit falls during the mango season in late March to August then you should try this delicious fruit. The many species of Keralan bananas – small, green, red, long – are also very tasty. There are also tender green coconuts, prized as a refreshing drink and for the cream which is scooped out and eaten as a snack. The yellow flesh of the ripened jack-fruit is considered a delicacy and is sold in little leaf bowls (don't drink water at the same time or you will end up with stomach ache). Guavas, pineapples and papayas are all available in season.

Rice, curries and fish served on a banana leaf

To Help You Order...

I would like...	**Nan venam...**
no chilli	**mulaku illa**
to eat	**tinnuka**
to drink	**kutikkuka**
water	**vellam**
yes	**untu**
no	**illa**

Basic Food Vocabulary...

annam or **coru**	rice
kaytacakka	pineapple
kolikkari	chicken
mampalam	mango
mannakkari	mango pickle
min	fish
moru	buttermilk
mulaku	chilli
murinnakka	drum stick
mutta	egg
narannakkari	lime pickle
nentrappalam	
or **ettappalam**	banana
palu	milk
parippu	lentils
pavaykka	bitter gourd
rotti	bread
sasyam	
or **paccakkri**	vegetables
tairu	yoghurt/curd
tenna	coconut
valappalam	plantain
valutananna	aubergine
ventaykka	okra

HANDY TRAVEL TIPS

An A–Z Summary of Practical Information

A

ARRIVAL

Once through customs the visitor is often besieged by porters, taxi drivers and others. Choose one porter and stick to him. There is a system of paying porters a fixed amount per piece of baggage before leaving the terminal: a tip of Rs5, once the bags are aboard the taxi or bus, is sufficient. If a travel agent or a friend is meeting you, he or she may be waiting outside the building. Some major hotels operate courtesy buses and there are also offical, pre-paid taxi stands.

B

BEGGING

Visitors to Kerala will encounter quite a few people asking for alms, especially in the cities, around holy shrines and on railway journeys. Many of these beggars are physically disabled and they have few other options for survival. Although you should use your discretion, giving small amounts of money (one or two rupees) will be gratefully received and will generally be helping someone out. Try and give discreetly as you might attract unwanted attention. If you are unsure about whether to give or not, it is fine to follow what other people around you are doing.

BUDGETING FOR YOUR TRIP

Return flights to India from the UK vary widely in price but you can expect to pay between £400 and £650 for a ticket to and from Thiruvananthapuram or Chennai.

Whilst India is a cheap place for Western visitors, if you want to stay in some of the classier places then you will find prices are not much different from the UK. Good, cheap accommodation is available from around Rs500 (£8), with the more expensive five-star hotels reaching at least £200–300 per night.

Food is cheap, however, with local meals setting you back as little as Rs30 (around 40 pence), and you would be hard pushed to pay more than Rs1,500 each (around £20) in even the most expensive establishments.

Entrance fees are invariably charged for archaeological sites, museums and galleries. These are usually nominal (around Rs2–5). However, for sites that attract a lot of tourists you might well find that there is an Indian fee (of the usual Rs2–5) and a 'foreign tourists' fee' which will be considerably more (anything from Rs200–500).

Other costs, such as for transport, are considerably cheaper than in the West.

C

CLIMATE

Kerala is warm throughout the year, except in the hill ranges. But the region can also be very wet, especially if the monsoons are good. Average temperatures in the plains range from 23–29°C (73–85°F) in Kerala and 19–31°C (66–88°F) in Lakshadweep. Hill station temperatures tend to range from about 10–18°C (50–65°F).

The hottest part of the year is from April–June, just before the southwest monsoon. Temperatures on some days can reach over 40°C (110°F). Kerala can be very humid. The monsoons begin around 10 June and can last well into October. Kerala and Lakshadweep are lashed by seasonal monsoon rains.

From October to February/March the weather is mainly dry, with temperatures ranging from 18–24°C (64–75°F) and hill stations even registering a low of 4°C (39°F). Kerala, however, does get rain at this time of the year; the northeast monsoon being most active from mid-October to early December. Kerala and Lakshadweep in the monsoon are experiences in themselves, but sea-bathing is ruled out by rough seas at this time of the year.

	J	F	M	A	M	J	J	A	S	O	N	D
Av. Temp.												
°C	31	32	33	32	31	29	29	29	30	30	30	31
°F	88	90	91	90	88	84	84	84	86	86	86	88
Min Av.												
°C	22	23	24	25	25	24	23	22	23	23	23	23
°F	72	73	75	77	77	75	73	72	73	73	73	73
Rainfall												
mm	20	20	43	122	249	331	215	164	123	271	207	73
in.	0.79	0.79	1.69	4.8	9.8	13	8.4	6.4	4.8	10.6	8.1	2.8

CLOTHING

It is best to wear cotton when travelling in South India. Avoid synthetics. Cotton shirts, blouses and skirts are inexpensive and easily available in all towns and cities. Remember to bring underwear (especially bras) and swimwear. In winter, a light sweater might be necessary as the early mornings can be a little chilly. Comfortable footwear is essential. 'Trekking' sandals are excellent for wearing in India as they are tough and provide good protection to your feet. Teva and Reef are good brands.

For their own convenience, women should not wear sleeveless blouses, mini skirts and short or revealing dresses. Cover up – it's a good idea in the Indian sun anyway – locally available *shalwar kamiz* (also known as a *churidar*), a long tunic top worn over loose trousers, are ideal.

CUSTOMS

Customs procedures have recently been simplified. Visitors fill in declaration forms on the plane, and then proceed to the relevant red or green channels. Keep the slip in your passport for when you disembark. Tourists seldom have any trouble. Occasionally, customs officials ask to see one suitcase at random and make a quick check.

Currency declaration At present, forms for bringing in amounts of cash in excess of US$10,000 must be completed at customs on arrival.

Duty-free imports These include 200 cigarettes (or 50 cigars), 0.95 litres (1 pint) of alcohol, a camera with five rolls of film and a reasonable amount of personal effects, including binoculars, laptop, sound-recording instruments, etc.

Professional equipment and high-value articles must be declared or listed on arrival with a written undertaking to re-export them. Both the list and the articles must be produced on departure. As this formality can be a lengthy process, allow extra time, both on arrival and at departure. For unaccompanied baggage or baggage misplaced by the airline, make sure you get a landing certificate from Customs on arrival.

Exports Export of antiques (over 100 years old), all animal products, and jewellery valued at over Rs2,000 (in the case of gold) and Rs10,000 (in the case of articles not made of gold) are banned. When in doubt about the age of semi-antiques, contact an office of the Archaeological Survey.

Prohibited articles These include certain drugs, live plants, gold and silver bullion, and coins not in current use. All checked luggage arriving at the larger airports is X-rayed before reaching the baggage collection area in the arrival hall.

D

DEPARTURE

It is absolutely essential to reconfirm your reservations for all outward-bound flights at least 72 hours before departure, especially in the peak season, when most of the flights are overbooked. Security procedures can be intensive and time-consuming, so allow at least two hours for check-in.

An airport/seaport tax is charged on departure and must be paid prior to check-in (check the cost with your airline at the time of booking). Do ensure that the name of your outward-bound carrier is endorsed on the tax receipt. For visitors with entry permits, exit endorsements are necessary from the office where they were registered. Should a stay exceed 180 days, an income tax exemption certificate must be obtained from the Foreign Section of the Income Tax Department in Delhi, Mumbai, Kolkata or Chennai.

Remember before you leave that there is a departure tax of Rs750 (Rs550 for neighbouring SAARC countries) for all international departures. This should be included in your ticket, but make sure you check with your airline or on your ticket, where it should be marked.

DISABLED TRAVELLERS

Although disability is common in India, there are very few provisions for wheelchairs and special toilets. The roads are full of potholes and kerbs are often high and without ramps. If you have difficulty walking, it may be hard to negotiate street obstacles, beggars, or steep staircases. On the other hand, Indians will always be willing to help you in and out of buses or cars, or up stairs. Taxis and rickshaws are cheap and the driver, with a little bakshis, will probably help. You could employ a guide who will be prepared to help with obstacles. Another option is to go with a paid companion.

In the UK, Holiday Care, 7th Floor, Sunley House, 4 Bedford Park, Croydon, Surrey CR0 2AP (tel: 0845 124 9974; <www.holiday-care.org.uk>), could put you in touch with someone. Some package-holiday operators cater for travellers with disabilities, but ensure that your needs have been understood before making a booking. Contact an organisation for the disabled for further information.

E

ELECTRICITY

The voltage system in India is 220V AC, 50 cycles. DC supplies also exist, so check first. Sockets are of the two round-pin variety normally, but do vary. Take a universal adaptor for British, Irish and Australasian plugs. American and Canadian appliances will need a transformer. Electricity supplies may be irregular, especially during the summer, as demand often outstrips supply. Power being switched off at local distribution points is known as 'load shedding'.

EMBASSIES, CONSULATES AND HIGH COMMISSIONS

In Chennai
British Deputy High Commissioner, 24 Anderson Road, Nungambakkam, tel: (044) 2827 3136–7, fax: (044) 2826 9004.
Consulate of Canada, Chamber 2, Business Centre, The Residency Towers, Thyagaraja Road, tel: (044) 2815 1445, fax: (044) 2815 7029
US Consulate, 220 Anna Salai, tel: (044) 2827 3040.

In Delhi
Australian High Commission, Australian Compound, 1-50G Shantipath, Chanakyapuri (P.O. Box 5210), tel: (011) 5139 9900, fax: (011) 5149 4491.
British High Commission, Shantipath, Chanakyapuri, New Delhi, tel: (011) 2687 2161 (24 hrs), fax: (011) 2687 0065.
Canadian High Commission, 7–8 Shantipath, Chanakyapuri, New Delhi (P.O. Box 5207), tel: (011) 2687 6500.
Irish Embassy, 13 Jor Bagh, tel: (011) 2462 6714.
New Zealand High Commission, 50N Nyaya Marg, Chanyakapuri, New Delhi, tel: (011) 2688 3170.
US Embassy, Shantipath, Chanakyapuri, New Delhi, tel: (011) 2419 8000, fax: (011) 2419 0017.

Indian Missions Abroad
Australia, High Commission of India, 3–5 Moonah Place, Yarralumla, Canberra ACT-2600, tel: (616) 273 3774/273 3999, fax: (616) 273 3328/273 1308, <www.highcommissionofindiaaustralia.org>.
Canada, High Commission of India, 10 Springfield Road, Ottawa, Ontario KLM 1 C9, tel: (613) 744 3751–3, fax: (613) 744 0913, <www.hciottawa.ca>.

Great Britain, High Commission of India, India House, Aldwych, London WC2B 4NA, tel: (0891) 880 800 (24-hours recorded visa information); (020) 7836 0990 (specific visa enquiries); (020) 7836-8484 (general), <www.hcilondon.org>.

US, Embassy of India, 2107 Massachusetts Avenue NW, Washington DC 20008, tel: (202) 939 7000, fax: (202) 939 7027, <www.indianembassy.org>.

EMERGENCIES

Generally speaking, India is a safe place to travel, but a tourist is a natural target for thieves and pickpockets, so take the usual precautions and keep money, credit cards, valuables and passport in a money belt or pouch well secured with a cord around your neck. A protective hand over this in a crowded place could save you a lot of heartache and hassle.

Do not leave belongings unattended, especially on a beach. Invest in good strong locks (available in India) for your bags. Chaining luggage to the berth on a train, or to your seat on a bus, is another precaution that travelling Indians often take. Watch your luggage carefully, especially during loading and unloading.

Credit card frauds do exist so make sure that shops and restaurants process your card in front of you.

Another sensible precaution is to keep a photocopy of your passport and visa, traveller's cheque numbers and receipts, ticket details, insurance policy number and telephone claims number, and some emergency money in a bag or case separate from your other cash and documents. If you are robbed, report the incident immediately to a police station (be patient, this can take hours).

ENTRY REGULATIONS

Tourist visas for all nationalities are issued for three or six months from the date of issue (not entry). It is preferable to take a multiple-entry visa, in order to have the option of visiting a neighbouring country.

Get a visa from the embassy or high commission in your country of residence, rather than risk the complications and delays involved in applying for one in neighbouring countries.

Tourist visas cannot be extended; you must leave the country and re-enter on a new one. It may be difficult to apply for a new visa from neighbouring countries. Five-year visas are also issued to business people and students. In addition to visas, special permits are required for certain areas, while other areas are out of bounds to foreigners altogether *(see Restricted and Protected Areas below)*.

If you stay for more than 180 days, before leaving the country you must have a tax-clearance certificate. These can be obtained from the foreigner's section of the income tax department in every city. Tax-clearance certificates are free, but take bank receipts to demonstrate that you have changed money legally.

Restricted and Protected Areas Lakshadweep: only Agatti, Bangaram and Kadmat are open to foreign tourists. Kavaratti may be used for transiting.

ETIQUETTE

● Removing one's shoes before entering someone's house, a temple or mosque is essential. Overshoes are provided in some places of worship at a nominal cost and stockinged feet are usually permissible.

● The *namaskaram* greeting with joined hands is the Indian form of salutation and its use will be appreciated, though men, especially in the cities, will not hesitate to shake hands with you if you are a man. A handshake would even be appreciated as a gesture of special friendliness.

Most Indian women would be taken aback at the informality of interaction between the sexes common in the West, and physical contact between men and women is to be avoided. Men should not shake hands with a woman (unless she first offers to).

● Avoid taking leather goods of any kind into temples as these can often cause offence.

● Always walk around religious shrines clockwise.

● Photography is prohibited inside the inner sanctum of many places of worship. Do obtain permission before using a camera. Visitors are usually welcome to look around at their leisure and can sometimes stay during religious rituals. For visits to places of worship, modest clothing is essential. In mosques, women should cover their head and arms and wear long skirts. A small contribution to the temple donation box *(hundi)* is customary.

● In private, visitors are received as honoured guests and your unfamiliarity with Indian ways will be accepted and understood. When eating with your fingers, remember to use only the right hand.

● Avoid pointing the soles of your feet towards anyone as this is considered a sign of disrespect. Don't point with your index finger: use either your extended hand or your chin.

● Central Government has passed a law banning smoking in all public places, and this has now been enacted by most State governments.

G

GAY AND LESBIAN TRAVELLERS

Homosexuality is still a taboo subject for many Indians. Sexual relations between men are punishable with long prison sentences and cruising in public could come under public disorder laws. There is no similar law against lesbians.

While general attitudes are discriminatory, things are changing slowly, and at least the issue of gay and lesbian rights is starting to be discussed, due in no small part to Deepa Mehta's 1998 film *Fire*, which depicted an affair between two married women, and the 2004 film *Girlfriend*. Attacks on cinemas by the religious right brought counter demonstrations onto the streets of major cities.

However, gay and lesbian travellers should be discreet and avoid any public displays of affection (as should heterosexual couples). On the plus side, hotels will think nothing of two men or women sharing a room.

GETTING AROUND

Air Travel Indian (previously Indian Airlines <www.indian-airlines.
nic.in>) has one of the world's largest domestic networks. The reservations system has been improved by the introduction of computers, and tickets can now be booked online. For travel during the peak season (September–March), try and make reservations in advance as flights are usually heavily booked.

The Discover India fare, valid for 21 days of travel all over the country, and the Tour India Scheme, valid for 14 days and limited to six flight coupons, are both particularly attractive. These tickets must be purchased abroad, or paid for in India using foreign currency.

Air India (<www.airindia.com>) carries domestic passengers on its linking flights between Mumbai and Delhi, Kolkata, Chennai and Bangalore. These flights leave from the international terminals in the respective cities. The privately operated airlines Air Deccan (a low-cost and web-based carrier; <www.airdeccan.net>) and Jet Airways (<www. jetairways.com>), which has a particularly good reputation, fly on many domestic routes.

Boats Kerala operates a regular passenger-boat system on its canals and lagoons. A number of services operate from Alappuzha and Kollam (formerly Alleppey and Quilon), including the popular backwater trip between the two. Boats run daily (by the Water Transport Department or Alleppey Tourism). The trip lasts up to eight hours depending on the route. There is also a boat service to and from the Lakshadweep islands from Kochi (see <www.lakport.nic.in>).

Buses Almost every part of Kerala is connected by an extensive and well-developed bus system (<www.keralartc.com>) with the railway stations being the natural hubs for both local and regional services. Some of the more rural routes are serviced by noisy dilapidated vehicles, but an increasing number of deluxe and air-conditioned expresses ply the trunk routes. There are many parts of the state where the bus service is the only means of public transport. Most baggage is carried on the bus roof, so all bags should be locked and checked on at intermediate stops. Almost all cities have a bus service. However, it is generally preferable to use taxis or three-wheeled "auto-rickshaws".

Taxis and Rickshaws Chauffeur-driven cars, costing around £10–15 a day, can be arranged through tourist offices, hotels or local car-rental firms. Taxis are both air-conditioned and non-air-conditioned (cheaper and sometimes more comfortable). Charges vary, ranging from Rs325 for eight hours and 80km (50 miles) to Rs450 for an air-conditioned car. For out-of-town travel, there is a per-km charge, usually between Rs2.30–Rs3 per km in the plains (in the hills this rate is often Rs6 per km), with an overnight charge of Rs100. Package tours, sold by travel agencies and hotels, include assistance, guides and hotel accommodation, in addition to taxi charges.

When taking a taxi or bus into town from the airport, it is advisable to change money in the arrival hall. Enquire at the information desk for the going rate for a journey to your destination before getting into the taxi; and make sure the meter is 'down' before you embark. It is alright to share a taxi even if the destination may not be the same (although it should be in the same area). In some cities taxis have fare charts which, when applied to the amount on the meter, give the correct fare. There is often a night surcharge of 10 percent between 11pm and 6am and a rate of Rs1 to Rs2 per piece of baggage.

The most convenient, and classically Indian, way of getting around town is by rickshaw. These come in two types: a cycle rickshaw (a tricycle with a seat for two people on the back), and a motorised three-wheeler known as an 'auto' (to cut down on pollution some of these have now been converted to run on CNG, compressed natural gas).

Autos are, like taxis, supposed to use a meter. Meter rates are subject to periodic changes, and extras for late-night journeys etc., which the driver should show you on a card. In popular tourist spots, during rush hour and bad weather, you may find it impossible to persuade the drivers to use the meter. A tactic that might work is to offer 'meter plus ten' (the cost plus Rs10). If not, you'll have to negotiate the fare. After a short while in the country you will get a feel for what is acceptable and, given that as a relatively well-off foreign tourist you are expected quite reasonably to pay a little more, what is not.

In many places it is common for auto drivers to suggest that, for a fixed amount, they take you around the sites for a whole day. This can be convenient and, if you bargain well, good value. The fare for three-wheelers is about half that of taxis.

Railways Rail travel is safe and comfortable. Indian Railways has a number of different classes, of varying degrees of comfort. In descending order of price, they are: first class AC, very comfortable with lockable cabins of four berths each; AC II tier, partitions arranged in groups of 6 berths with curtains that pull across to provide privacy; AC III tier, partitions with groups of 9 berths, the middle berths fold down for sleeping; AC chair car; first class (now rare) non-AC but with ceiling fans, with lockable cabins of four berths each and one cabin of two berths halfway down each carriage; sleeper class, partitions of 9 berths with ceiling fans; and second class, unreserved with no berths and hard seats. Reservations are required for all classes other than second class. In the summer months it is best to go AC. When the weather is cooler then first class non-AC can be an excellent option as it is possible to see the passing countryside without having to stare through the darkened windows of AC. All carriages have both Western and Indian-style toilets.

Most stations now have very efficient computerised booking counters from where you can book any ticket for any route. To buy your ticket you must first fill out a Reservation Requisition Form, which will be available from one of the windows in the booking office. Reservations may be made up to 60 days in advance and cancellations (for which you will need to fill in the same form as for a reservation) can be made right up until the time of departure. If reservations are not available then certain trains have a tourist quota that may be available. Other options are to take a waitlisted ticket or the more assured reservation against cancellation (RAC). Tatkal trains (marked with a 'T' in timetables) have a certain number of reservations held back, which become available one day in advance for an extra charge.

The concise but comprehensive *Trains At A Glance* is probably the most useful timetable for foreign tourists. This, and local timetables, should be available from railway stations. All this information (and more, including fares and details of special trains and passes) can be found on the Indian Railways websites: for general information <www.indianrailways.gov.in>; for timetables and the current status of trains and your ticket <www.indianrail. gov.in>; and <www.irctc.co.in> to buy tickets online (you will need to register, and delivery and collection of tickets is only available in certain cities; see the website for details). See also the site of the Konkan Railway <www.konkanrailway.com> and that of the Southern Railway <www.srailway.com>.

GETTING THERE

By Air The vast majority of visitors arrive in India by air. Mumbai and Chennai airports are the major entry points. Other international airports include: Thiruvananthapuram, with flights to and from the Gulf region, the Maldives and Sri Lanka. Kozhikode and Kochi are airports with limited international air access and Customs and immigration facilities, and are not international airports in the real sense of the term. They have a number of scheduled flights to and from the Gulf region. Discounts are often available during the off-peak season, so it is worth making enquiries.

Many long-haul flights arrive between midnight and 6am, apparently to suit the night landing regulations of European and East Asian cities but, in reality, to help a full plane taking off in the thin air of an Indian summer.

Check with the airline to confirm your booking well in advance. NB: It is advisable to check in for flights to and from India as early as possible as planes are often full and/or overbooked. All airports have left-luggage facilities. Porters and licensed, pre-paid taxis are available from all airports. Airport banks are open 24 hours for currency change.

By Sea A few cruise ships do call in at ports such as Cochin, but India is not a regular cruise destination. Some freighters offer passage to India and excellent accommodation is still available. Great Eastern Shipping (<www.greatship.com>), Lloyd Triestino (<www.lloyd triestino.it>) and the Shipping Corporation of India (<www.shipindia. com>) have sailings to and from Mumbai, Kolkata and Chennai.

H

HEALTH

Diarrhoea Usually caused by low-level food poisoning, this can be avoided with a little care. When you arrive, rest on your first day and only eat simple food; well-cooked vegetarian dishes and peeled fruits are perhaps best. An upset stomach is often caused by eating too many rich Indian meat dishes (usually cooked with vast amounts of oil and spices) and failing to rest and let your body acclimatise.

Drink plenty of fluids but never drink unboiled or unfiltered water. When in doubt, stick to soda, mineral water, or aerated drinks of standard brands. Avoid ice as this is often made with unboiled water. All food should be cooked and eaten hot. Don't eat salads and always peel fruit.

Immobilising drugs such as loperamide (Imodium) and atropine (Lomotil) can be useful, particularly if you have to travel. The most important thing to do in cases of diarrhoea and/or vomiting is to rehydrate, preferably using oral rehydration salts.

Dysentery and Giardia These are more serious forms of stomach infection and should be suspected and treated if the diarrhoea lasts for more than 2 days. Dysentery is characterised by diarrhoea accompanied by the presence of mucus and blood in faeces. Other symptoms include severe stomach cramps and vomiting. Bacillic dysentery comes on quickly and is usually accompanied by fever. It may clear up by itself but its usual treatment is a course of antibiotics such as ciprofloxacin or tetracycline. Amoebic dysentery has a slower onset and will not clear up on its own. If you suspect you have amoebic dysentery you should seek medical help as it can damage the gut. The usual cure is a course of metronidazole (Flagyl) three times daily with food for 7 days. You must not drink alcohol when taking metronidazole. Giardia is a similar infection caused by a parasite. Like amoebic dysentery it comes on slowly and its symptoms include rotten-egg belches as well as diarrhoea. Giardia will not clear up on its own and will recur; its treatment is the same as for amoebic dysentery.

Fungal infections Prickly heat is a common complaint caused by excessive perspiration. Try to keep the skin dry by using talcum powder and wearing loose-fitting cotton clothes. Fungal infections are also common, especially during the monsoon, and can be treated by exposure to the sun and/or by the application of anti-fungal cream.

Malaria This moquito-borne disease is very serious and potentially fatal. There are two common strains in India, *P. falciparum* and *P. vivax*, both carried by the Anopheles mosquito. Symptoms are similar to acute flu (including some or all of fever, shivering, diarrhoea and muscle pains) and an outbreak may come on as much as a year after visiting a malarial area. If malaria is suspected then medical attention should be sought as soon as possible.

Prophylaxis is essential. The usual anti-malarial protection for India consists of a combination of daily proguanil (Paludrine) and weekly chloroquine (Avoclar, Nivaquin). These are now bought across the counter in the UK, and your pharmacist will advise you on the correct dosages. An alternative drug is mefloquine (Lariam), taken weekly. However, this should not be taken by people with a history of epilepsy or mental illness. In the UK mefloquine is only available as a private prescription. A newly approved drug is the atavoquone-proguanil combination marketed as Malarone, recommended for areas of chloroquine resistance.

The best, and only certain protection against malaria is not to get bitten. Sleep under a mosquito net impreganted with permethrin, cover up in the evenings and use an effective insect repellent such as DEET (diethyltoluamide). Burning mosquito coils is also a good idea.

Sun exposure The dangers of sunburn are now well-publicised. Cover up and use a high-factor sunscreen, even if it is cloudy. The power of the sun is obvious on the plains and in tropical India and overexposure can also lead to the two conditions below:

● Heat exhaustion is common, indicated by shallow breathing, rapid pulse, pallor, and is often accompanied by leg cramps, headache or nausea. The body temperature remains normal. Lying down in a cool place and sipping water mixed with rehydration salts or plain table salt will prevent loss of consciousness.

● Heatstroke is more serious, and more likely to occur when it is both hot and humid. The body temperature soars suddenly and the skin feels dry. The victim may feel confused, then pass out. Take them quickly to a cool room, remove their clothes and cover them with a wet sheet or towels soaked in cold water. Call for medical help and fan them constantly until their body temperature drops to 38°C (100°F).

Vaccinations No inoculations are legally required to enter India, but it is strongly advised that you get inoculations against typhoid, hepatitis A, polio, diptheria, tetanus and meningitis A, C, W and Y. You may need to show proof of a yellow fever inoculation if arriving from an infected area. Other diseases against which vaccinations might be considered, particularly for longer trips, include rabies and Japanese B encephalitis. There is no vacccination against Dengue fever, occasionally contracted in India. The only protection is to avoid being bitten.

L

LANGUAGE

The language of Kerala is Malayalam (with a few pockets of Tamil speakers in the tea planting areas, Palakkad District and to the south of Thiruvananthapuram). Malayalam is essentially a Sanskritised version of Tamil and many of the basic words and phrases are mutually intelligible between the two languages.Malayalam is generally held to be the most challenging of the South Asian languages for non-native speakers, and is very quickly spoken. However, visitors will have little trouble being understood as almost everyone has at least a smattering of English.

Some basic Malayalam phrases

Hello/Goodbye	**Namaskaram**
Please	**Deyavu Cheytu**
Thank You	**Nanni**
OK	**Sari**
Yes	**Untu**
No	**Illa**
Where is…?	**Evide anna…?**
I would like…	**Nan venam…**
Where is the toilet?	**Tailet evide?**
I am from…	**Nan… ninnu**
How much?	**Enta villa?**
How are you?	**Sukmano?**
What?	**Enta?**
Where?	**Evide?**
I don't understand	**Mansilla illa**
What is your name?	**Ninte peru entanu?**
My name is…	**Enthe peru aanu…**
Right	**Vallate**
Left	**Edade**

Numbers

One	**Onnu**
Two	**Randu**
Three	**Munnu**
Four	**Nallu**
Five	**Anch**
Six	**Aru**
Seven	**Ezhu**
Eight	**Ettu**
Nine	**Ompatu**
Ten	**Pattu**

M

MAPS

Short of getting hold of detailed government maps (many of which are not available to the public), good and accurate maps of Kerala are few and far between. One of the best widely available maps is in the Eicher *India Road Atlas* (available from <www.indiamapstore.com>).

MEDIA

Newspapers and Magazines   The English-language newspaper *The Hindu* (<www.hinduonnet.com>), established well over 100 years ago, is published as a regional edition. A serious, well-edited newspaper with a national slant to the news, *The Hindu* is one of the best English-language newspapers in Asia. The local editions carry regional news, and it carries a comprehensive diary of events every day. It also publishes the exemplary fortnightly news magazine *Frontline* (<www.frontlineonnet. com>). *The Indian Express* (<www.indian-express.com>), another daily also published in Kerala, has a lighter style than *The Hindu* but is still well written and with good reports. Kerala does not have an English daily of its own, though its Malayalam-language dailies are among the newspapers with the highest circulation in the country.

Other news magazines with a national reach include *India Today* (<www.india-today.com>), *Outlook* (<www.outlookindia.com>) and *The Week* (<www.the-week.com>). There are also excellent general-interest magazines such as *Sanctuary* (<www.sanctuaryasia. com>), which specialises in South Asian natural history. There are several glossy women's magazines in English, including *Femina* (<www.femina india.com>) and Indian editions of *Cosmopolitan* and *Elle*.

Television and Radio   Doordarshan is the government TV company and broadcasts programmes in English, Hindi and regional languages. Local timings vary, but generally the news in English can be heard daily at 7.50am and 9.30pm. Satellite television is available almost everywhere, including the Star TV's network incorporating the BBC World Service and MTV. NDTV is a local 24-hour news channel that provides good coverage of Indian news and politics. Other stations include Channel V (a local youth-orientated music channel) and Zee TV (Hindi). There are channels showing sport, American soaps and sitcoms and English-language movies. Up to 50 channels can be picked up, given the right equipment.

All India Radio (AIR) broadcasts on the short-wave and medium-wave. The frequencies vary, so check with your hotel.

MONEY

All encashments of traveller's cheques and exchange of foreign currency used to have to be recorded on a currency declaration form, or receipts kept as proof of legal conversion. The laws have eased, but some businesses and hotels may still insist. Visitors staying more than 180 days will have to produce proof of encashment of traveller's cheques or exchange of currency for income tax exemption and show they have been self-supporting.

Indian currency is based on the decimal system, with 100 paise to the rupee. Coins are in denominations of 10, 20, 25 and 50 paise and 1, 2 and 5 rupees. Notes are in 10, 20, 50, 100 and 500 rupee denominations. Indian rupees may not be brought in nor taken out of the country. Exchange rates fluctuate against other currencies but currently there are approximately Rs70 to £1 sterling.

Credit cards are increasingly accepted by hotels, restaurants, large shops, tourist emporia and airlines. It is preferable to have a well-known card such as American Express, MasterCard or Visa. A number of banks will now issue rupees against a Visa card and Amex issues rupees or traveller's cheques to cardholders against a cheque at their offices. More conveniently, ATMs that issue cash against a variety of cards are found in many places. The ATMs of local banks may only issue cash against their own cards so try and find a machine of an international bank.

O

OPENING TIMES

Banks Open from 10am–2pm weekdays, 10am–noon Saturday for most foreign banks and nationalised Indian banks (of which the State Bank is the largest). Some banks operate evening branches, while others remain open on Sunday and close on another day of the week, and some open 9am–1pm. All banks are closed on national holidays, on 30 June and 31 December.

Government offices Officially 9.30am–6pm Monday to Friday, but most business is done between 10am and 5pm with a long lunch break.

Post Offices Open from 10am–4.30pm Monday to Friday, and until 12 noon on Saturday. In most of the larger cities, the central post office is open until 6.30pm on weekdays, 4.30pm on Saturday. On Sunday some open until noon. Major telegraph offices are open 24 hours.

Shops Open from 10am–7pm. Some shops close for lunch. Although Sunday is an official holiday, different localities in major cities have staggered days off so that there are always some shopping areas open.

P

POLICE

The Indian police have an unnenviable reputation for corruption and brutality, although this is likely to be aimed more at locals than tourists, who will have little need to come into contact with them. When you will need them is in the unlikely event that you have anything stolen and you need a police report in order to claim on your insurance. If this does happen, go to the nearest police station and obtain a First Information Report (FIR). Be prepared for a long wait as this can take some time to compile.

POST

The internal mail service is efficient in most areas. It is advisable to personally affix stamps to letters or postcards and hand them over to the post office counter for immediate franking rather than to post them in a letterbox. Indian stamps do not stick very well so make sure you use the pot of gum that is almost always available.

Sending a registered parcel overseas is a complicated and time-consuming process. Most parcels should be stitched into cheap cotton cloth and then sealed (there are people outside or close to major post offices offering this service). Two customs forms need to be completed. Once the parcel has been weighed and stamps affixed, make sure it is franked and a receipt of registration is issued. Important or valuable material should be registered.

PUBLIC HOLIDAYS

Sunday is the official weekly holiday throughout South India, but a few private establishments might close on Friday. Other compulsory holidays are:

26 January (Republic Day)
1 May (May Day)
15 August (Independence Day)
2 October (Mahatma Gandhi's Birthday)

R

RELIGION

Kerala is 52 percent Hindu with two large minority communities, the Muslim community (known as the Mapillas) at 26 percent, and the Christians (the majority of whom are Syrian Orthodox) at 19 percent. Relations between the three groups are generally very good.

T

TELEPHONES

Calling from hotels can be extremely expensive, with surcharges up to 300 percent, so check rates first. Mobile telephones are widely used in India and your own phone may well work while you are there. Privately run telephone services with international direct-dialling facilities are very widespread. Advertising themselves with the acronyms STD/ISD (standard trunk dialling/international subscriber dialling), they are quick and easy to use. Some stay open 24 hours a day. Both national and international calls are dialled direct. Some booths have an electronic screen that keeps time and calculates cost during the call. Prices are similar to those at official telecommunications centres. To call India from abroad, dial the international access code, followed by 91 for India, the local code less the initial zero, then the number.

Indian telephone numbers change often and although those in the book have been checked carefully they may well change in the future. NB. Indian telephone numbers are now all 10 digits long (including the area code minus the initial zero). The vast majority of numbers now start with a '2'. If you encounter an old-style number (i.e. eight digits long) add a '2' to the beginning and it should work. US international access codes are: MCI 000 127; Sprint 000 137; and AT&T 000 117.

E-mail and the internet are now very popular and widely available. All large cities, and many smaller places, have internet cafés or similar places where you can surf the net or send e-mails. Charges are usually by the minute or hour, and are usually around Rs60 per hour.

TIME ZONE

India is 5½ hours ahead of Greenwich Mean Time.

TIPPING

There is no harm expressing your appreciation with a small tip. Depending on services rendered and the type of establishment, this could range from Rs10 upwards. In restaurants, the tip is customarily 10–15 percent of the bill. Leading hotels add a 10 percent service surcharge and tipping in such places is optional. For taxis or autos, 10 percent of the fare or leaving the change, if not substantial, would be adequate

TOILETS

Toilets in most mid-price and expensive hotels will be Western-style, generally very clean, and supplied with toilet paper. In cheaper places and on trains and in public places such as railway or bus stations you will encounter Indian-style squat toilets. With these you are expected to wash your bottom with your left hand, using the pot *(lota)* provided to pour the water onto your hand and to rinse down the ceramic section set into the floor. Using an alcohol-based hand gel (available from chemists) afterwards will kill any residual bacteria and help you feel more hygenic.

TOURIST INFORMATION

The Kerala Tourist Development Corporation (KTDC) has its head office in Thiruvananthapuram (Mascot Square, tel: 0471-272 5213). It also has two Tourist Reception Centres, one beside the Hotel Chaithram, Thiruvananthapuram (tel: 0471-233 0031), the other on Shanmugham Road, Ernakulam (tel: 0484-235 3234). They run tours, which can be a useful way of seeing local sights if you are short of time, and can help you book accommodation. They also have a useful website (<www.ktdc.com>).

W

WATER

Many water supplies in India are contaminated and are a common source of disease for travellers who have no immunity to water-borne bacteria such as giardia. Bottled water is available. However, there is no guarantee that this is safe and, perhaps more importantly, it is extremely bad for the environment (India is accumulating an enormous plastic bottle mountain). It is much better to carry your own water bottle and fill it from safe water sources (the best is boiled water). This is not always available and portable water filters are an excellent solution. Those made by Katadyn (<www.katadyn.com>) are considered the best.

WEBSITES AND INTERNET CAFÉS

There are numerous places offering internet access in Kerala, from hotels (which can be expensive) to small 'cafés' (a room divided into cubicles). Connections from Kerala can be slow but are improving all the time. Charges are very reasonable and shouldn't be more than around RPS 60 per hour.

Useful websites

KTDC (<www.ktdc.com>).

Kerala Tourism (<www.keralatourism.org>).

Department of Forests and Wildlife (<www.keralaforest.org>).

Tour India (<www.tourindiakerala.com>).

Malayala Manorama (<www.manoramaonline.com>).

commercial sites (<www.kerala.com>), (<www.newkerala. com>) and (www.keralaonline.com>).

WEIGHTS AND MEASUREMENTS

The metric system is uniformly used all over India. Precious metals, especially gold, are often sold by the traditional *tola*, which is equivalent to 11.5 grams. Gems are weighed in carats (0.2 grams). Financial outlays and population are usually expressed in *lakhs* (100 thousand) and *krores* (100 *lakhs* or 10 million).

WOMEN TRAVELLERS

'Eve-teasing' is the Indian euphemism for sexual harassment. Take the normal precautions such as looking out for yourself on crowded local public transport (crowds are a haven for gropers). Do not wear clothes that expose legs, arms and cleavage; *shalwar kamiz* are ideal, and a shawl is handy to use as a cover-all when required.

More serious sexual assaults on tourists are rare and tend to occur in popular tourist areas, but in case something should happen, call for help from passers-by. On the up-side, there are 'ladies-only' queues at train and bus stations, and 'ladies-only' waiting rooms at stations and compartments on trains.

Recommended Hotels

Accommodation in Kerala is varied to say the least; it runs the full gamut from the very cheap and rather unsavoury to the hideously expensive with every conceivable luxury thrown in. Between these two extremes are some lovely places to stay. The indigenous five-star chains (such as the Taj Group) are extremely well-run, but luxury does not come cheap and you will pay well over £100 per night in high season. Perhaps some of the best places to stay are in homestays (a rising trend in Kerala where families are throwing open their often charming traditional houses to visitors), which also tend to have the best food you will taste on your trip.

The hotel listings below have been placed in the following categories which are for a double room (AC where available) in high season, including taxes.

$$$$$	over Rs4,000
$$$$	Rs3,000–4,000
$$$	Rs1,700–3,000
$$	Rs700–1,700
$	below Rs700

ALAPPUZHA

Alleppey Prince Hotel $$$ *A.S. Road; tel: (0477) 224 3752, fax: (0477) 224 3758.* Decent, clean, air-conditioned rooms, restaurant and pool, in a long-established hotel. *Kathakali* dance performances are occasionally staged and backwater tours can be organised from here.

Emerald Isle Heritage Villa $$$ *Kanjooparambil–Manimala-thara; tel: (0477) 270 3899, mobile: 94470 77555; <www.emerald islekerala.com>.* A highly recommended, peaceful retreat. Four guest rooms with lovely 'outdoor' bathrooms in a traditional house set in idyllic tropical surroundings. Excellent traditional Keralan meals and considerate, friendly service. Twelve km (7 miles) from Alappuzha; call in advance so the boat is waiting for you at the jetty to take you over to the island. Evening boat trips can be arranged as well as cruises on *kettuvallams*.

Kayaloram Heritage Lake Resort $$$–$$$$ *Punnamada; tel: (0477) 223 2040, fax: (0477) 223 1871; <www.kayaloram.com>.* A peaceful resort 4km (2½ miles) from Alappuzha (free transfer at 11am and 1pm). Individual Keralan-style wooden cottages, as well as a restaurant and pool. Stays can also be arranged in *kettuvallams* – traditional boats.

KTDC Yatri Nivas $ *Motel Aram Compound, A.S. Road; tel: (0477) 224 4460, fax: (0477) 224 4463; <www.ktdc.com>.* Good-value air-conditioned rooms (very cheap non-AC accommodation) in a government-run guesthouse.

La Casa del Fauno $$$$$ *Muhamma, Aryakkara; tel: (0478) 286 0862; <www.casadelfauno.com>.* A very classy homestay, about 8km (5 miles) from Alappuzha. The rooms are spotless and attractive in a kitschy-minimalist sort of way. The facilities on offer include, among others, boat hire, *Ayurvedic* treatments and a swimming pool.

Raheem Residency $$$$$ *Beach Road; tel: (0477) 223 0767, mobile: 94470 82241; <www.raheemresidency.com>.* A beautiful colonial villa dating from 1868 now converted into a chic and luxurious heritage hotel. The rooms are delightful, with period furniture. The staff are attentive without being pushy and there is a lovely pool. It is not far from Alappuzha beach.

ATHIRAPALLI

Rainforest $$$ *Kannamkuzhy; tel: (0480) 276 9062; <www.avenue center.com>.* This peaceful resort has superb views over the waterfalls and surrounding forests. The rooms and facilities are rather basic but it is the location that counts.

BEKAL

Gitanjali Heritage $$$ *Panayal; tel: (0467) 223 4159; <www. gitanjaliheritage.com>.* This is a wonderful place to base yourself. Mr Jagannathan and his family are very welcoming and their 70-year-old home, a traditional *kodoth* house, is beautifully maintained. It is set in a delightful garden and the food is excellent. Mr Jagannathan is also a mine of information on the local *Teyyam* dances. This is a highly recommended retreat.

GURUVAYUR

Vrindavan Tourist Home $ *Next to KSRTC Bus Stand, West Nada; tel: (0487) 255 4033.* A rather sweet and well-maintained budget lodge that mainly caters to pilgrims. The staff are welcoming and the rooms are clean and extremely good value.

KANNUR

Royal Omars Hotel $$–$$$ *Thavakkara, opposite Bharat Petroleum; tel: (0497) 276 9091.* A flash, modern business hotel near the station. Remarkably good value comfortable rooms and facilities.

KOCHI-ERNAKULAM

Abad Plaza $$$ *M.G. Road, Ernakulam; tel: (0484) 238 1222, fax: (0484) 237 0729; <www.abadhotels.com>.* A good, modern hotel with clean rooms in central Ernakulam. There is a pool and a decent restaurant serving seafood.

Adams Hotel $$ *South Junction, Ernakulam; tel: (0484) 237 7707.* A good-value hotel above Pizza Hut, very convenient for the railway station. Clean rooms and efficient service.

The Avenue Regent $$$$ *39/2026 M.G. Road, Ernakulam; tel: (0484) 237 7977, fax: (0484) 237 5329; <www.avenueregent. com>.* A modern business hotel with very comfortable rooms. The hotel restaurant is very good (try the buffet lunch) and the **Loungevity** bar is one of the best in the state.

The Brunton Boatyard $$$$$ *Calvetty Road, Fort Cochin; tel: (0484) 221 5461, fax: (0484) 221 5562; <www.cghearth.com>.* A luxury hotel in a splendid location, built in the style of early Portuguese and Dutch colonial architecture. Elegant and beautifully appointed rooms and bathrooms. A good restaurant serves local dishes recreated from historical recipes.

Casino Hotel $$$$ *Willingdon Island; tel: (0484) 266 8221, fax: (0484) 266 8001; <www.cghearth.com>.* Comfortable hotel with a highly recommended seafood restaurant. Very clean and tasteful rooms (nice touches such as cosmetics in small terracotta pots in the bathrooms), and a good pool. A little way from the centre of Ernakulam but convenient buses go to M.G. Road.

Delight Tourist Resort $$–$$$ *Parade Ground, Fort Kochi; tel: (0484) 221 6301; <www.delightfulhomestay.com>.* A quiet little guesthouse with spotless rooms right in the centre of Fort Kochi. Comfy beds, a lovely garden and an extremely helpful travel desk.

Malabar House Residency $$$$$ *1/268–9 Parade Road, Fort Cochin; tel: (0484) 221 6666, fax: (0484) 221 7777; <www.malabarhouse.com>.* One of the best luxury hotels in Kerala, set in a refurbished 300-year-old house within the fort area. The rooms are comfortable and furnished with antiques, there is an inviting plunge pool, and the food in the outdoor restaurant is excellent. Often booked up so make reservations well in advance.

SAAS Tower Hotel $–$$ *Cannon Shed Road, near Boat Jetty, Ernakulam; tel: (0484) 236 5319, fax: (0484) 236 7365.* This good-value hotel has decent if smallish rooms. The attached restaurant has good Indian food.

Taj Malabar $$$$$ *Malabar Road, Willingdon Island; tel: (0484) 266 6811, fax: (0484) 266 8297; <www.tajhotels.com>.*

One of the best hotels in the state; try and get a room in the old wing, which is more atmospheric. There are also good restaurants – especially the one where you sit outside on the point of the island overlooking the harbour – and there's a pool too.

Woodlands $$ *M.G. Road, Ernakulam; tel: (0484) 238 2051, fax: (0484) 238 2080; email: <woodland1@vsnl.com>*. A comfortable hotel with clean, excellent-value air-conditioned rooms (it's cheaper for non-AC rooms) and a good vegetarian restaurant.

YHA $ *NGO Qrts Junction, Thrikkakra; tel: (0484) 242 2808, fax: (0484) 242 4399; <www.yhaindia.com>*. A bit out of the way behind Ernakulam Junction, but clean, good value and quiet. Meals are available.

KOLLAM

Government Guest House $ *Ashramom; tel: (0474) 274 3620*. Formerly the British residency, on Ashtamudi Lake. Very atmospheric, it has five spacious rooms, and food, if ordered in advance. Backwater trips may be arranged from here (the boat will pick you up from the jetty across from the garden).

KTDC Yatri Nivas $ *Ashramom, Guest House Compound; tel: (0474) 274 5538; <www.ktdc.com>*. This large, government-run hotel has good-value, basic rooms and is situated beside the lake (opposite the jetty).

Hotel Sudarshan $$ *Paramesvar Nagar, Hospital Road; tel: (0474) 274 4322, fax: (0474) 274 0480; <www.hotelsudarshan.com>*. Clean, largish air-conditioned rooms with attached bath and hot water. There is also a restaurant and snack bar.

KOTTAYAM

Hotel Aida $$ *Aida Junction, M.C. Road; tel: (0481) 256 8391, fax: (0481) 256 8399; <www.hotelaidakerala.com>*. Good-value, comfortable rooms, all with bath and hot water. There is a restaurant serving Indian dishes.

Coconut Lagoon $$$$$ *Vembanad Lake; tel: (0484) 266 8221; <www.cghearth.com>.* One of the finest resorts in Kerala, about 10km (6 miles) from Kottayam and only accessible by boat. The facilities are first class, including the *Ayurvedic* treatments, and the rooms are tasteful and luxurious.

KTDC Aiswarya $$ *Thirunakkara; tel: (0481) 258 1440, fax: (0481) 256 5618.* Pleasant rooms in a government-run hotel, with optional air conditioning and cable TV. The hotel also has a decent restaurant.

Vembanad Lake Resort $$ *Kodimatha; tel: (0481) 236 1633, fax: (0481) 236 0866.* Located 3km (2 miles) from the town. Comfortable cottages in gardens by the lake. A good restaurant on a houseboat serves *tanduri* and seafood dishes.

KOVALAM

Coconut Bay $$$$$ *Vizhinjam; tel: (0471) 248 0566; <www.coconutbay.com>.* A well-run and quiet resort, just behind the beach, set out in small bungalows. The staff are discreetly attentive and the *Ayurvedic* package here is extremely good.

Lagoona Davina $$$$ *Pachallur; tel: (0471) 238 0049, fax: (0471) 238 2651; <www.lagoonadavina.com>.* Peaceful resort, close to Pozhikkara Beach, run by Englishwoman Davina Taylor. The attractive rooms have four-poster beds, and there is good food, *Ayurvedic* massage and yoga classes.

The Leela Kovalam $$$$$ *tel: (0471) 248 0101, fax: (0471) 248 1522; <www.theleela.com>.* Striking hotel complex (previously the Kovalam Ashok), designed in part by Charles Correa. The hotel now includes the Halcyon Castle, summer palace of the Maharajas of Travancore. Expensive but exceptionally luxurious, with a great pool and in a superb location.

Maharaju Palace $$ *Tel: (0471) 0031-299 372 597; <www.maharajupalace.nl>*. A Dutch-owned hotel (book through the Netherlands) close to the lighthouse. Very pleasant and quiet and only 30m (100ft) from the beach.

Hotel Neelakanta $$–$$$ *Lighthouse Beach; tel: (0471) 248 0321, fax: (0471) 248 0421; <www.hotelneelakantakovalam.com>*. This reasonably priced hotel is right on the beach front. The rooms have huge windows and balconies, all of which gives you a great view over the sea.

Hotel Rockholm $$–$$$ *Lighthouse Road; tel: (0471) 248 0306, fax: (0471) 248 0607; <www.rockholm.com>*. Pleasant hotel at the end of Lighthouse Beach. The spotless rooms have great views and there is a good restaurant.

Hotel Sea Face $$$$ *N.U.P. Beach Road; tel: (0471) 248 1835, fax: (0471) 248 1320; <www.hotelseaface.com>*. A popular hotel close to the beach. Pleasant, clean rooms, friendly staff, as well as a good restaurant and pool.

Surya Samudra Beach Garden $$$$$ *Tel: (0471) 226 7333, fax: (0471) 248 0413; <www.suryasamudra.com>*. An expensive and exclusive resort with accommodation in relocated traditional houses. It's 8km (5 miles) from Kovalam in a wonderful, quiet location overlooking the sea.

Taj Green Cove Resort $$$$$ *G.V. Raja Vattapara Road; tel: (0471) 248 7733, fax: (0471) 248 7744; <www.tajhotels.com>*. The Taj group doing what it does best, well run and with low-key luxury. Very comfortable rooms and cottages set in lovely grounds, and with a superb pool.

KOZHIKODE

Alakapuri Hotel $ *Moulana Mohamed Ali Road; tel: (0495) 272 3451, fax: (0495) 272 0219*. An excellent-value colonial-style guesthouse. The large rooms with bath are full of character. The restaurant serves good Indian food.

Kadavu $$$$$ *N.H. Bypass Road, Azhinjilam; tel: (0495) 283 0570, fax: (0495) 283 0575; <www.kadavuresorts.com>*. Beautifully located hotel, 14km (8½ miles) from Kozhikode. The comfortable rooms and suites all have a spectacular view over the river, and there is good food in the restaurant.

Malabar Palace $$ *Manuelsons Junction, G.H. Road; tel: (0495) 272 1511, fax: (0495) 272 1794; <www.malabarpalacecalicut. com>*. A modern hotel that is a comfortable mid-budget choice with good air-conditioned rooms. Friendly service and a very efficient front desk. There is also an excellent restaurant.

MUNNAR

Blackberry Hills $$$–$$$$ *Bison Valley Road, Pothamedu; tel: (04865) 232 978, fax: (04865) 232 965; <www.blackberryhills india. com>*. A group of cottages 3km (2 miles) out of town in an idyllic location. Well kept, with stunning views, the staff can also arrange treks in the surrounding countryside.

Edassery East End $$$ *Temple Road; tel: (04865) 230 451, fax: (04865) 230 227; <www.edasserygroup.com>*. This large hotel has comfortable double rooms in the main building, and a series of cottages in the well-maintained grounds. Good value for its location and facilities, this is one of the best hotels in the town itself.

Isaac's Residency $$$ *Top Station Road; tel: (04865) 230 501*. A comfortable, modern hotel close to the centre of town. The rooms are spacious and well maintained, and the ones at the front of the building have excellent views. The in-house restaurant is not bad.

The Olive Brook $$$$ *In the Tata Tea Estate, Pothamedu; tel: (04865) 230 588; <www.olivebrookmunnar.com>*. These two bungalows set high above the town are a lovely retreat. The staff are great and there are cooking demonstrations in the evening. Highly recommended.

THIRUVANANTHAPURAM

Hotel Chaithram $$ *Central Station Road, Thampanoor; tel: (0471) 233 0977, fax: (0471) 233 1446; <www.ktdc.com>*. A clean, good-value KTDC hotel opposite the railway station. Some rooms have air conditioning and attached baths. There is a good restaurant on the ground floor. It is often full so book in advance.

Greenland Lodging $–$$ *Aristo Road; tel: (0471) 232 3485*. A long-established and decent, budget hotel with clean rooms. Very convenient for the railway and bus stations if you are making an early start.

Hazeen Tourist Home $ *Off Aristo Road; tel: (0471) 232 5181*. Clean, but very basic rooms in a quiet hotel.

Hotel Highland Park $$ *Manjalikulam Road, Thampanoor; tel: (047) 223 8800, fax: (0471) 233 2645*. A newish hotel with both AC and non-AC rooms at good rates. The rooms are well maintained and there is a decent vegetarian restaurant.

Mascot Hotel $$$ *P.M.G. Junction; tel: (0471) 231 8990, fax: (0471) 231 7745; <www.ktdc.com>*. Pleasant, quiet, renovated hotel, originally built to house British officers during World War I. In a quiet location with a good restaurant.

The Muthoot Plaza $$$$ *Punnen Road; tel: (0471) 233 7733, fax: (0471) 233 7734; <www.sarovarhotels.com>*. The city's top business hotel, with very comfortable rooms and good facilities.

Hotel Prathiba Heritage $ *Dharmalayam Road; tel: (0471) 233 6442*. Very central with clean and safe rooms in a friendly hotel. Filtered water available.

Residency Tower $$$–$$$$ *South Gate of Secretariat, Press Road; tel: (0471) 233 1661, fax: (0471) 233 1311; <www.residency tower.com>.* A modern, comfortable hotel with good facilities. There are good restaurants and a rooftop pool. Good value for what's on offer.

The South Park $$$$ *M.G. Road; tel: (0471) 233 3333, fax: (0471) 233 1861; <www.thesouthpark.com>.* A swish hotel with a flash lobby, aimed at the business market, with reasonable rooms.

THRISSUR

KTDC Yatri Nivas $ *Near Indoor Stadium; tel: (0487) 233 2333, fax: (0487) 233 2122; <www.ktdc.com>.* A good budget option, government-run with clean rooms. Snacks are available.

Mannapuram Hotel $$ *Kuruppam Road; tel: (0487) 244 0933, fax: (0487) 242 7692.* A modern but attractive hotel with comfortable, well-priced and clean rooms. Well run with a good restaurant.

Ramanilayam Government Guest House $ *Palace Road; tel: (0487) 233 2016.* Strictly speaking for visiting officials only. Large suites with balconies in a colonial mansion. Food available to order in advance. Excellent value.

VARKALA

Taj Garden Retreat $$$$$ *Near Government Guest House, Janardana Puram; tel: (0472) 260 3000, fax: (0472) 260 2296; <www.tajhotels.com>.* A luxurious resort hotel close to Varkala's superb beach. There are great views from its hilltop position. Good restaurants and pool.

Villa Jacaranda $$$$ *Temple Road West; tel: (0470) 261 0296; <www.villa-jacaranda.biz>.* Spotless and nicely designed rooms in a modern guesthouse. The surrounding gardens are quite beautiful and the views of sunset over the sea breathtaking.

VYTHIRI

Green Magic Nature Resort $$$$$ *Book through: Tour India, P.O. Box 163, near S.M.V. High School, M.G. Road, Thiruvananthapuram; tel: (0471) 233 0437, fax: (0471) 233 1407; <www.tourindiakerala. com>.* Accommodation is in either a wonderful treehouse or in cottages set in the heart of a pristine rainforest. This is an eco-resort in the true sense of the term (they use bio-gas and solar power, serve organic food and only natural cosmetics are allowed). Not cheap, but it is a unique experience.

LAKSHADWEEP

Bangaram Island Resort $$$$$ *Book through: Casino Hotel, Willingdon Island, Kochi; tel: (0484) 266 8221, fax: (0484) 266 8001; <www.cghearth.com>.* Visitors are transferred by boat from Agatti to this peaceful luxury resort. All-inclusive board and lodging, but bottled water is extra and charged at a slightly shocking mark-up rate (make sure you have enough cash to cover extras at the end of your stay). The water in the bathrooms smells strongly of sulphur, but it is safe. Accommodation is in simple huts; meals take the form of a buffet with lots of fresh fish. The friendly and helpful staff hold a barbecue on the beach one night a week. There are facilities for snorkelling and scuba diving, and there's a bar on the beach (again, drinks are not included in the price of the package).

Kadmat Cottages $$$$$ *Book through: Lacadives, Lakshmi Niwas, 43/2051 K Colony, Kochi; tel: (0484) 220 6766; <www.lacadives.com>* A lovely, if simple, resort on a fabulous lagoon. Transfer is by boat from Agatti. Accommodation is in small cottages with air conditioning and attached bathrooms. The price includes all meals, but alcohol is not allowed. There is a small shop selling basics such as toiletries, snacks and soft drinks. The swimming, and particularly the diving, is excellent. Dive packages are available, including those for beginners, or you can book single dives by the day (for an extra fee).

Recommended Restaurants

Most of the best restaurants are to be found in hotels, and where a hotel has a particularly good place to eat this has been mentioned in the listings on *pages 127–37*. If you are looking for a pleasant night out then these should be your first option. Booking is not generally necessary for restaurants, though it might be wise to phone those in the luxury hotels beforehand.

However, these may not be the best places to find local dishes. To find these you should head for local 'hotels' (both veg and non-veg) as local eating places are often called in South India. 'Meals' places are generally excellent, cheap and very clean. Look for places with a high lunchtime turnover (the traditional time for the day's big meal) to find the best food. 'Meals' usually come in the form of a *thali*, literally a 'tray' with a pile of rice in the middle and small pots containing different vegetable and *dal* dishes, as well as some curd, around the edge. Most are open for lunch and dinner, usually from around noon–3pm, and then 6–10.30pm, though cheaper places are generally open all day.

Street food from stalls, provided it is fresh and cooked in front of you, can be very good and tasty. Snacks range from *chana dal* and *puris* to omelettes laden with green chillies to freshly cooked *paratha*. As with most things, use your common sense and only buy from stalls that appear hygienic.

ALAPPUZHA

Arun *Komala Hotel, tel: (0478) 224 3631* Good vegetarian meals in a small restaurant attached to a hotel.

Indian Coffee House *Mullakai Main Road, tel: (0478) 225 3862, also on Palace Road, tel: (0478) 226 2050.* Coffee and basic meals from the state-wide chain; a good place for breakfast.

GURUVAYUR

Indian Coffee House, *Kizhakkenada, tel: (0487) 255 6654*. A dependable fall back in this town which is mostly given over to feeding pilgrims.

KOCHI-ERNAKULAM

Bimby's/Southern Star *Sanmukam Road, Ernakulam*. Bimby's is a great place for cheap Indian fast food. The Southern Star upstairs does very good and reasonably priced sit-down meals.

Canopy Coffee Shop *Abad Plaza Complex, M.G. Road, Ernakulam*. Tasty continental and fast food – a good place for breakfast. Open all day.

Caza Maria *6/125 Jew Town Road, Mattancherri, Kochi, tel: (0484) 222 5678*. This restaurant on the first floor of a historic building has been beautifully decorated. The food is an imaginative mixture of Indian and European dishes on a menu that changes daily.

The Cocoa Tree *The Avenue Regent, M.G. Road, Ernakulam*. A great modern coffee shop attached to the hotel. Good coffee, light meals and excellent pastries. Open until 1am.

Gokul Restaurant *M.G. Road, Ernakulam, tel: (0484) 237 5605*. An excellent place for South Indian meals and snacks, the *dosas* and *uttapams* are particularly good.

Indian Coffee House *Cannon Shed Road, Ernakulam, tel: (0484) 236 1061, also at Darbar Hall Road, tel: (0484) 235 4724, M.G. Road and at the Kerala High Court Campus, tel: (0484) 239 4435*. Good snacks and coffee in a somewhat run-down building not far from the main jetty.

Pandhal *M.G. Road, Ernakulam*. A very clean restaurant that serves up good North Indian and tasty Keralan dishes.

KOLLAM

Indian Coffee House *Main Road, Chinnakkada, tel: (0484) 275 1329*. Decent snacks and coffee from this popular chain.

Sri Suprabathan *Clock Tower*. A cheap and cheerful vegetarian place, with tasty food.

KOTTAYAM

Indian Coffee House *T.B. Road, tel: (0481) 256 3064, also at M.L. Road, tel: (0481) 256 3169 and the Medical College, tel: (0481) 259 9848*. The usual non-vegetarian snacks and good coffee. Convenient for the bus station.

Thali Restaurant *Homestead Hotel*. Decent vegetarian meals served on the eponymous metal tray.

KOVALAM

Kovalam has a plethora of eating places, most of them much of a muchness. They tend to specialise in grilled or fried fish, served with chips. You first of all choose your fish, making sure that it is fresh (check inside the gills and make sure the eyes are not too glassy). Some places to try include the **Sea View Restaurant** (at the northern end of Lighthouse Beach), the **Swiss Café Restaurant** and **Fusion** (both on Lighthouse Beach and both with decent views).

German Bakery *South End of Lighthouse Beach, tel: (0471) 248 0179*. Something of a Kovalam institution, the bakery-cum-restaurant sells strudel and bread, as well as dishing up a good selection of Thai and European dishes (mostly pasta).

The Lobster Pot *Above Ashok Beach*. An excellent viewpoint on top of the cliff and under the coconut palms. Decent enough Indian food, but the location is better.

KOZHIKODE

Kalpaka Tourist Home, *Town Hall Road*. Reasonable Indian food. Conveniently near the railway station.

Sagar *I.G. Road*. A very popular restaurant with locals, sometimes you have to queue to get a table. However, the wait is worth it as the Indian food is excellent.

Woodlands *G.H. Road*. A good, and cheap, vegetarian meals hall in the centre of town.

THIRUVANANTHAPURAM

Annapoorna *Pazhavangadi, opposite the Ganesh Temple*. A good meals place with an air-conditioned first floor 'family room'. The *dosas* and *uttapams* are particularly good and the fresh fruit juices (make sure you order without ice) are also worth a try.

Arul Jyothi *M.G. Road, opposite the Secretariat*. A very clean meals hall with excellent food. This is some of the best vegetarian food in the city. Good for juices.

Casa Bianca *96 M.P. Appan Road, Vazhuthacaud, tel: (0471) 233 8323*. This lovely café and restaurant run by Ingrid, a Swede settled in Thiruvananthapuram, is a little out of the ordinary for the city. A well-designed interior is the setting for very tasty Italian and Indian food (the pizza is excellent). Open daily 11am–10pm.

Coffee Beanz *Magnet, Thycaud*. A modern café, opposite the women's college, serving excellent coffee and snacks such as chips and sandwiches. A popular hang-out for students and young people. Open Mon–Sat 11am–10pm, Sun 9am–10pm.

Indian Coffee House *Maveli Café, Central Station Road, tel: (0471) 233 3527, also at many other locations, including M.G. Road, tel: (0471) 247 7595, the Secretariat Campus, opposite the*

Botanical Gardens, tel: (0471) 251 8301, Sanmukam Beach, tel: (0471) 250 5779. City landmark, beside the bus stand. Great coffee and snacks served in spiral building designed by Laurie Baker. A good place for breakfast or a late-night snack.

Park Field Gardens *Cotton Hill, Vazhuthacaud.* A pleasant restaurant serving good Indian and international dishes. The combination meals, with a wide variety of Indian dishes, are particularly good.

Hotel Sri Bhadra and Hotel Sree Padmanabha *Opposite the temple tank, Fort.* A pair of decent vegetarian restaurants serving meals – *dosas* and the like – with not much to choose between them. They both have good views of the temple from the first floor and can be very pleasant in early evening.

THRISSUR

Hotel Anupam *The Round.* Decent vegetarian meals, with plenty of tasty extras, not far from the north gate of the temple. 'Meals' are served on the first floor.

Indian Coffee House *Round South, tel: (0487) 242 1794, also at C.B.D., tel: (0487) 233 1749, Kuruppam Road, tel: (0487) 242 7470, and K.A.U. Mannuthi.* Another set of places from the Keralan cooperative, all serving the usual good coffee and reasonable selection of snacks.

VARKALA

Like Kovalam, Varkala too has a whole string of restaurants lined up along the sea front. Most of them have great views out to sea and the food is all much of a standard (the usual combination of North Indian dishes, noodles and some seafood). Near the road try the **Somatheeram Beach Restaurant** or the **Sea Face** (both on Main Beach, Papanasam), or the slightly more upmarket **Marine Palace** just above.

INDEX